FOREST PARK

Awe and wonder at the "Grandfather Tree," Jay Trail. (Hike 13)

Forest Park

Exploring Portland's
Natural Sanctuary

Marcy Cottrell Houle

Oregon State University Press   Corvallis

Generous support from the Oregon Parks Foundation Fund of Oregon Community Foundation, the John and Shirley Byrne Fund for Books on Nature and the Environment, and the Houle family helped make publication of this book possible.

Cataloging-in-publication data available at the Library of Congress.
ISBN 978-0-87071-222-7 (paperback); ISBN 978-0-87071-223-4 (ebook)

∞This paper meets the requirements of ANSI/NISO Z39.48-1992 (Permanence of Paper).

Maps by Erik Goetze, ArtofGeography.com

Oregon State University Press
121 The Valley Library
Corvallis OR 97331-4501
541-737-3166 • fax 541-737-3170
www.osupress.oregonstate.edu

Oregon State University Press in Corvallis, Oregon, is located within the traditional homelands of the Mary's River or Ampinefu Band of Kalapuya. Following the Willamette Valley Treaty of 1855, Kalapuya people were forcibly removed to reservations in Western Oregon. Today, living descendants of these people are a part of the Confederated Tribes of Grand Ronde Community of Oregon (grandronde.org) and the Confederated Tribes of the Siletz Indians (ctsi.nsn.us).

To Catherine Thompson
whose devotion to the preservation of the natural world,
in particular, her love of Forest Park,
has given a gift to all of us and to future generations.

Along the hills northwest of Portland, "there are a succession
of ravines and spurs covered with remarkably beautiful
primeval woods. . . . It is true that some people look upon
such woods merely as a troublesome encumbrance standing
in the way of more profitable use of the land, but future
generations will not feel so and will bless the men who were
wise enough to get such woods preserved. Future generations,
however, will be likely to appreciate the wild beauty and the
grandeur of the tall fir trees in this forest park . . . its deep
shady ravines and bold view-commanding spurs, far more
than do the majority of the citizens of today, many of whom
are familiar with similar original woods. But such primeval
woods will become as rare about Portland as they now are
about Boston. If these woods are preserved, they will surely
come to be regarded as marvelously beautiful."

   —John Charles Olmsted and Frederick Law Olmsted
   Jr., Report of the Park Board, Portland, Oregon, 1903

Contents

Acknowledgments

This book does not belong to me. It is a true collaboration of amazing people—scientists, historians, resource specialists, and experts in a wide variety of fields—coming together with a shared passion:

We treasure Forest Park.

Many of these people have spent years studying different aspects of the park. I can't say enough about their willingness to share their knowledge, answer my voluminous questions, and lead me to new sources, and then take the time to review the chapters—sometimes repeatedly—to make sure the information presented is precise and as up-to-date as possible.

Their efforts reflect something that E. O. Wilson wrote in one of his last books, *In Half-Earth: Our Planet's Fight for Life.*

The clear lesson of biodiversity research is that the diversity of species, arrayed in countless natural ecosystems on the land and in the sea, is under threat. Those who have studied the database most carefully agree that human activity, which has raised the species extinction rate a thousand times over its prehuman level, threatens to extinguish or bring to the brink of extinction half of the species still surviving into this century. Yet there remain scattered around the world many reservoirs of Earth's biodiversity, from a few acres in area to authentic original wildernesses with areas in excess of many thousands of square kilometers. Almost all of these last domains of the natural living environment are under some degree of threat or other, but *they can be saved for future generations if those alive today have the will to act on their behalf.*

The people I acknowledge on the next page demonstrate that will. That is why I say this book belongs to all of us. It is with humble and true appreciation I want to thank each of you who has contributed so much:

David Barrios, Forest Park Ranger, Portland Parks and Recreation.
Leah Bendlin, Mycologist, Oregon Mycological Society.
Michele Blackburn, Conservation Biologist with the Xerces
    Society.
Dr. Scott Burns, Professor Emeritus of Engineering Geology at
    Portland State University.
Char Corkran, Wildlife and Amphibian Consultant.
John Deshler, Wildlife Biologist, Author, and Pygmy Owl specialist.
Janet Drake, Portland Audubon Society.
Dr. Jerry Franklin, Professor Emeritus at the University of
    Washington's College of the Environment.
Laura Guderyahn, Ecologist and Herpetologist, Bureau of
    Environmental Services.
Dave Helzer, Terrestrial Biologist, Portland Bureau of
    Environmental Services.
John Houle, Civil Engineer and Watershed Specialist, Portland
    Bureau of Environmental Services.
Paul Ketchum, Watershed Ecologist, Portland Bureau of
    Environmental Services.
Kim Kosmas, Senior Public Education Officer, Portland Fire and
    Rescue.
Paul S. Majkut, Attorney-at-law.
Renee Myers, Executive Director, Forest Park Conservancy.
Chet Orloff, Historian, Founder of Museum of the City,
    Executive Director Emeritus, Oregon Historical Society.
Mark Peters, Environmental Specialist, Portland Bureau of
    Environmental Services.
Kendra Peterson Morgan, Natural Areas Supervisor, Portland Parks
    and Recreation.
Hannah Prather, PhD, Lichenologist, Reed College.
Chris Prescott, Watershed Ecologist, Portland Bureau of
    Environmental Services. (And a special shout out to the entire
    BES Westside Watersheds Team!)
Don Proth, Historian for Portland Fire and Rescue.
Becky Schreiber, Director of Volunteer Programs, Hoyt Arboretum.
Gerald Scrutchions, Educator, Board member, Hoyt Arboretum.
Elaine Stewart, Senior Natural Resources Scientist, METRO.

Jade Ujcic-Ashcroft, Avian Biologist, Portland Bureau of
Environmental Services.

This book could never have been done without the tireless and devoted efforts of two incredible people: Erik Goetze, the superb, prize-winning cartographer whose maps of Forest Park are the very best available anywhere (and keep us from getting lost!), and John Thompson, MD, photographer and plant and lichen specialist, whose beautiful pictures that accompany this book reveal the true glory of Forest Park.

I also wish to thank OSU Press, specifically Micki Reaman (editorial, design, and production manager) and Tom Booth, who is indisputably the very best publisher possible. His belief in this book has been a terrific motivator. Our long years of friendship have always kept me going as a writer.

I am grateful to my friend and beautiful writer Kathleen Dean Moore for her wonderful foreword for this book.

Lastly, I want to thank my dearest family—Emily, Jennifer, Will, Jason, Lucy, Lilly, and Heidi. They love the outdoors and Forest Park as much as I, and I am so grateful we all enjoy sharing it together.

Finally, my deepest appreciation goes to the love of my life, John. For over forty years he has hiked these trails with me. He makes each step a wonderful life.

Foreword

In my family's experience, what makes a city great is its great forests. We gladly travel to Portland to walk the forested paths of the Oregon Zoo, the Portland Japanese Garden, the Portland International Rose Test Garden, and, of course, the winding, always climbing trails of Forest Park. The shade of the great green trees makes Portland one of the finest of the world's cities. That is a fact worth pondering: What can explain the value of the urban forest to our lives?

Of course, we treasure the forest for its *instrumental* values because it serves human purposes, providing material goods, ecosystem services, and cultural and psychological benefits. During the terrible heat dome, people paid attention to the cooling effect of the forest. We have read with some interest about the healthy effect of walking in a forest's quietude and piney scent, taking what the Japanese call a "forest bath." We know how ecologically essential it is to provide a habitat where wild creatures can thrive, and not only wild creatures, but hominids of the jogging, hiking, stroller-pushing, conversing, or contemplative kind. We understand the increase in property values next to a forest, which surprises us not at all. We understand as well that free and equitable access to flourishing forests serves justice and equal thriving. Forest Park cleans Portland's air and absorbs its greenhouse gases. And I will say this also about the responsiveness of a forest to human needs: When my husband was being treated at the Oregon Health Sciences University, I walked in Forest Park alone. Walking in the park—swept up in its green branches, its eagerness, its endless growth, its urgency toward life—gave me hope and strength.

As Marcy Houle tells us in her title, *Forest Park: Exploring Portland's Natural Sanctuary*, the forest is a refuge—for wildlife, yes, but also for people. "Sanctuary" comes to us from a time, some thousand years ago, when most crimes were punishable by death. The accused could flee to the refuge of the *sanctum sanctorum* of some churches, where they were sheltered and protected from the lethal cruelty of the law. Now, we can flee to forests, pursued not by mastiffs and bailiffs, but by the phone, the merciless laptop, the head-pounding pulse of traffic, the blinking, blinding lights, schedules, Zooms. For a time, in the forest, we are safely held by the calm and quiet of the dim cathedral light.

So I would argue also for the *spiritual* values of an urban forest—for what forests do for our spirits when we walk off the sidewalk onto soft duff trails that lead us under lichen-draped trees standing up to their knees in sword ferns, silvery with mist and birdsong.

What never fails to lift my spirits are the hemlock seedlings that grow in dark, spongy logs thrown down by some long-past storm in Forest Park. They bear spicy, lacy witness to the continuity of life. Nothing vanishes here, I could see for myself; everything is transformed into something even more beautiful. Now that my husband's health is stable again, he and I walk together in forests, happy for their evidence of the constancy of change and the immortality of substance. Every falling leaf assures us that, like the trees, we came from the earth and, when the time comes, we will be folded back into its arms.

We look for mushrooms, too, in Forest Park, searching not only under the ferns but up in the forks of the trees, where squirrels sometimes stash them. With white, thread-like webs of mycelia, they stitch pine squirrel to mushroom to Douglas-fir to beaked moss, piecing together the quilt that is the infinite interconnectedness of all life. This matters. The ecologist Aldo Leopold famously wrote, "All ethics so far evolved rest upon a single premise: that the individual is a member of a community of interdependent parts." As the nearby forest reminds us of the interconnectedness of all being, it affirms this first premise of our moral evolution and invites us to draw the conclusion: from the intricate, life-giving relationships that link the destinies of people and places grows a moral responsibility to care for the land.

The forests of Forest Park have grown to a great ripeness because they have not recently been cut or burned or trampled or harvested or taken as spoils or pink-flagged by researchers. If they have been altered by human influences, those influences have enhanced, or at least have not interrupted, the natural processes of succession. So here is proof of the possibility of human restraint, of the human capacity to live on the land without wrecking it. The presence of a healthy forest community within the city provides a vision of what the nearby wild can be, if it is allowed to grow to its full measure. It provides also a vision of what city-dwellers can be, if they are allowed to grow their full measure of humanity as members of a thriving biocultural community.

So let us welcome Marcy Houle's new guide to the trails of Forest Park, which invites us—and empowers us—to walk from the hot noise of the city into the cool quiet of the trees. With this new book, none of us will lose our way on the trail, but perhaps we will lose some of the tension in our shoulders, some of the anxiety in our hearts, and find a new way home.

Kathleen Dean Moore

Introduction

Awe and wonder.

Something so simple, profound, and necessary for our souls, yet in our frenzied world, so hard to find.

A visit to 5,200 acres of native forest can give us these feelings, however. Located in Portland, Oregon, is an outstanding protected urban park unlike any other in the United States. Located on a mountain ridge 1,000 feet high, one mile wide, and seven miles long, Forest Park overlooks the confluence of two of the major rivers of the West: the Columbia and Willamette. The Cascade Mountains can be viewed to the east; the Oregon Coast Range connects to the north and west. With an abundance of natural beauty to feed our spirits, relax our overtaxed minds, and infuse our physical being with renewed health, Forest Park affords a respite of tranquility for all who enter. For thousands of years, it was home to Chinookan peoples, Native Americans of the Pacific Northwest. In 1903, it was described by landscape architect John Olmsted as "marvelously beautiful." Then, in 1948, it was at last created to be a new kind of park, "a sanctuary for people and wildlife."

Today, Forest Park is the crown jewel of the Portland park system.

After studying Forest Park as an author and wildlife biologist over four decades, my appreciation of its value only continues to grow. From its beginning, the Portland City Council proclaimed that the major purpose of Forest Park is to provide "an undisturbed, natural forest and park environment for the quiet recreational enjoyment of the City of Portland." A half century later, it remains faithful to that goal, offering a place where our spirits can be touched by something greater than ourselves. In the past ten years, however, exciting research undertaken by scientists in a variety of fields reveals that Forest Park also bestows gifts with attributes even more far-reaching.

Remarkably, only minutes from a major metropolitan area, Forest Park acts as a *biodiversity reserve*. Studies show it functions as a model urban ecosystem of exceptionally high quality. There are several reasons why.

Forest Park supports essential habitat for numerous and diverse native plant and animal species. Currently, many of these species, including one

1

third of its birds, are listed as Special Status Species. These are animals that are at risk—experiencing declining numbers locally, regionally, and nationally. Forest Park serves as a wildlife reserve for many interior forest species and acts as an important stopover for migratory birds.

Forest Park's watersheds are the healthiest and the least altered from their historical conditions of any within the city of Portland. Its streams are found to have the richest macroinvertebrate communities of all streams in the city. It is a refuge for amphibians such as salamanders and red-legged frogs. It provides valuable habitat for pollinators. Its exceptional connectivity with the Coast Range enables movement of many species and allows better chances for regeneration to occur.

Forest Park is an example of the Pacific Northwest western hemlock forest community—an ecosystem unique among all temperate forests in the world. Its extensive forest canopy plays essential roles in Portland—filtering out pollutants, sequestering carbon emissions, and cooling a warming city.

In an era of ongoing and sometimes overwhelming loss of bird and mammal species, only to be exacerbated with dire ramifications of climate change, the significance of Forest Park as an urban biodiversity reserve cannot be overstated. Researchers understand this, stressing the importance that all of us become well-informed of the park's true worth as we look to the future of our city.

For these reasons, the time is right for a new book on Forest Park.

Forest Park: Exploring Portland's Natural Sanctuary is all about *discovery*—encouraging people of all ages and backgrounds, cultures, and ethnicities to encounter the beauty and wonders of Forest Park. This book is designed to reach out to everyone—offering experiences where they can feel included, safe, and welcome. It hopes to inspire personal explorations and connections to the natural environment of Forest Park, and to bring a fuller awareness of this treasure. To do so, it is presented in a new way to experience Forest Park—by themed hikes.

Twenty-one hikes will help people discover their own Forest Park experience and deepen their connection to nature. Beautiful photographs by John Thompson reveal many of the wonderful things we can see while on the trails. Excellent new maps, updated by award-winning cartographer Erik Goetze, accompany each hike. (Additional maps can be found at http://osupress.oregonstate.edu/book/forest-park.) Explorers can choose between Great Hikes for Families and Kids, Great Hikes for Wildflowers, Great Hikes for Birdwatching, Great Hikes to Get to Know Your Ecosystem, and Great

Hikes for Getting in Shape. Even better, do all of them, or set off on an All Trails Challenge to tackle all eighty miles of Forest Park trails! Through these adventures, visitors will learn fascinating information on Forest Park's geology, history, watersheds, vegetation, lichens and mosses, amphibians and reptiles, pollinators, and native wildlife. *Forest Park: Exploring Portland's Natural Sanctuary* is a compendium of the most up-to-date and comprehensive information available in a single resource about Forest Park.

Through the years, some people have asked how I can continue to be so absorbed in one place. But exploring Forest Park is not like just visiting one place over and over. Its beauty and rich biodiversity connect me with nature and refill me with awe and wonder. So my answer is quite simple, really.

Each time I enter this natural sanctuary is like the first time.

Geology of Forest Park

The geologic history of Forest Park has been a continuing drama predominantly characterized by several recurring themes: violent volcanic eruptions originating far to the east that flooded vast areas with thick basaltic lava flows; episodes when land surfaces were inundated and submerged by marine, lake, or river waters; periods of local volcanism; periods of faulting and folding; and, in between, long, relatively quiet periods when land-building subsided, and surfaces lay subject to erosion.

The oldest recorded geologic event in Forest Park began approximately 22 million years ago, during the late Oligocene and early Miocene, when the land that would one day become the city of Portland was submerged underneath an inland embayment of marine waters. Thick beds of siltstone and shale, accumulating to depths of several thousand feet, were deposited under water at this time. This fossil-rich deposit, referred to by geologists as the Scappoose Formation, is the oldest known formation underlying the West Hills of Portland and Forest Park. Deposition of sediment ceased, however, when the entire region was slowly uplifted, forcing the seas to retreat. Today in Forest Park this formation has no outcrops; it is totally buried.

Over the next few million years, the area experienced a time of quiet and stability, and the sedimentary marine beds partly eroded. The calm, however, belied what was about to happen in the east, an event that would, in retrospect, sculpt the Tualatin Mountain Range more than any other in its history.

Sixteen million years ago, in middle Miocene, intensive volcanic activity affected much of Oregon. Fissures in southeastern Washington and northeastern Oregon began erupting enormous quantities of fluid lava, sometimes pouring out hundreds of cubic miles of molten material that covered tens of thousands of square miles. These flows originated from one of the world's thirty-five "hotspots," where magma comes to the surface from the mantle. At the present time, the hotspot is under Yellowstone National Park.

As the lava cooled, it solidified and formed basalt, a heavy, fine-grained igneous rock. Vast plains of what geologists refer to as Columbia River Basalt stretched from Idaho to the Pacific coast. It flooded the Portland area, entering through an ancient Columbia River Gorge, and covered the underlying Scappoose Formation with over 1,000 feet of basalt. Today, approximately 700 feet of Columbia River Basalt forms the Tualatin Mountain Range and constitutes most of its bulk.

As the Miocene period progressed, the eruptions stopped, and for several million years weathering forces attacked the basalt, slowly decomposing exposed surface rocks into clay. During this period, the climate of the Portland area was tropical, and an extensive, reddish laterite crust, which is created under tropical conditions, formed on the exposed basalt.

Thirteen million years ago, another major disturbance rocked the region. At this time, the present-day Cascade and Coast Ranges were uplifted and formed, and the basalt land surface of Portland, which had originally been laid down nearly horizontally, was squeezed and folded. This rippling action formed valleys, geologically referred to as "synclines," that were separated by upfolded arches of layered rock, or "anticlines." This is evident in the Tualatin Mountain Range, which is an anticline separating two major synclines to the east and west—the Portland and Tualatin Valleys.

Between 3 and 10 million years ago, during the Pliocene, the valleys continued to settle and eventually filled to become great lakes of water. The lakes, in turn, were filled with silts, today known as Sandy River Mudstone, that buried the basalt surfaces of the lake bottoms. When at last the basins could hold no more, they breached and joined with a powerful, ancestral Columbia River, which then rushed in to dump its load of quartzite pebbles and granitic rocks (carried all the way from the Canadian Rockies) into the deformed, submerged valleys. These river deposits, known as the Troutdale Formation, overlie the Columbia River Basalt on side slopes in Forest Park at elevations of up to 600 feet.

As the Pliocene drew to a close, volcanic activity resumed, this time, however, on a regional scale. Dozens of small, isolated volcanoes, generated by underlying source vents, rose up like exclamation points across the land surface of the Portland area. Referred to as Boring Volcanoes, they erupted lava, which cooled to become gray, platy basalt. Boring Volcanoes were formed starting 2.5 million years ago just south of what today is Oregon City and ended 55,000 years ago with Beacon Rock. The 267,000-year-old cone above Cedar Hills is the most famous example. Several such volcanoes existed along the crest of Forest Park and poured out Boring Lava, a formation still visible in isolated sections along the ridge top and on the western slope of the Tualatin Mountain Range.

The final rock formation capping most of Forest Park was laid down during the last million years of the Pleistocene by the actions of two major forces, river and wind, operating in tandem. The pulsing Columbia River, working to excavate a major river valley, was continually whipped by the wind that over time picked up large quantities of yellowish-brown, fine-grained sediment called silt from the Columbia's floodplain and transported it to the south and west. Today this wind-deposited silt formation, known as Portland Hills Silt, covers the upper part of most of the West Hills of Portland; its greatest known thickness of fifty-five feet occurs on Forest Park's crest.

Geologic sculpting of Forest Park still continues with other forces influencing and altering its land configuration. The eastern flank of the Tualatin Mountain Range, a steep, straight, fifteen-mile ridge, is the result of a long fault that lies beneath present-day St. Helens Road. More recently modifying the surface of the West Hills of Portland, landslides have carved the major side slopes, and over the past one hundred years, have created major construction problems. Portland Hills Silt, overlying Columbia River Basalt, is an unstable formation when wet, and in an area of high seasonal rainfall, it has repeatedly proven to be a poor foundation material. Often landslides have resulted when the equilibriums of slopes blanketed by silt have been affected by excavation or construction. This seemingly detrimental condition, however, while causing chagrin in many an expectant and hopeful land developer, is a significant reason why Portland's Forest Park escaped development in the past and remains in its lovely natural state today.

History of Forest Park

> It is hoped the feeling of an extensive, uninterrupted forest sanctuary
> may ever be preserved.
>
> —Thornton Munger, a founder of Forest Park

The human history of Forest Park begins over 10,000 years ago in the early postglacial era with the arrival of the original inhabitants of Portland—Indigenous peoples who settled in a land of warming climate. Mountains and hillsides were becoming forested at this stage of geologic history, with spans of prairie interspersing the landscape. Later, 3,000 to 4,000 years ago, the climate modulated even more, becoming cool and moist; since then, much of the resources we know today have remained the same. The mountains cradling Portland were embellished with dense forests. River bottoms were adorned in a patchwork of grasslands, wetlands, and floodplains. The welcoming climate brought Indigenous people to the area, the Chinooks, who made it their home—a place they could rely on with the bountiful resources the land provided.

And the land was rich. Black-tailed deer abounded, as did grouse and multitudes of wild berries and acorns from stately oaks. Camas lily—a major food source—was abundant in nearby areas, as was wapato, growing plentifully on what would become known as Sauvies Island. Waterfowl frequented the lowland lakes and marshes. Herds of elk roamed the upland forests and wet meadows affording plentiful game. Majestic western red cedar trees cloaked the hills surrounding Portland, from which the Chinooks carved canoes, made clothing, and built shelter. And there were fish—an abundant supply of wild salmon—on which the people depended.

Archaeological research has recorded sites with artifacts on the Tualatin Mountain Range from as far back as 6,000 to 9,000 years ago. The joining of the two major rivers was known to be one of the most densely populated areas in Oregon. Several bands of Indigenous, Chinookan-speaking people, distinguished from each other by dialect and culture, lived in this land of abundant natural resources. Skilled elk hunters and fishers of salmon, the

Lower Chinook bands, which included the Lower, Wahkiakum, Willapa and Cathlamet bands, and the Clatsop Tribe, occupied the lower Columbia area. They developed long-standing social organizations and the land held deep spiritual significance for them.

In more recent history, Lewis and Clark recorded in 1805–1806 journals that approximately 4,000 Native peoples inhabited the lower Columbia River. Yet, as Lewis was also to record, their centuries-old Indigenous Chinook settlements had been transformed in the years before his arrival. He was informed by an afflicted older woman that many Chinooks had died from smallpox. Tragically, over the next thirty years, most members of the Indigenous tribes succumbed to imported diseases—measles, cholera, smallpox, and influenza—decimating the populations and their villages.

At the same time early in the nineteenth century, other factors were coming into motion. Euro-Americans began learning about the fertile river valley that lay tucked away in a remote corner of the Oregon Territory, and it spurred interest and speculation. Before long, pioneer travel increased up and down the Willamette River. Soon permanent settlements started to dot the landscape along the lower Willamette, beginning with the small communities of Linnton and Springville in 1843, and in 1845 the establishment of Portland farther upriver. Multiple donation land claims were given to settlers from 1850 to 1855. Along the plains to the west, additional towns arose, and with them the desire of farmers to find ways to transport their crops to the people and shipping docks located along the Willamette River. However, one major geologic feature stood in the way of the new settlers—an 1,100-foot forested ridge known as the Tualatin Mountain Range.

Early settlers quickly began widening routes that had long been used by the Indigenous peoples. By 1849, emigrants were turning them into passes, soon to be surveyed and made into county roads. Many of the names are still used today: Germantown Road, Springville Road, Cornell Road, Cornelius Pass. As the area continued to grow more populated, parcels of forest land adjoining the roads were quickly acquired.

By 1859, most of what is now Forest Park had been given away in Donation Land Claims to settlers. It was rapidly being logged. The virgin forest that had clothed the Tualatin Mountain Range for centuries was quickly exploited for firewood, building materials, sawlogs, and fuel for steamboats. Yet a remarkable concurrence was also originating around this time. In 1867, an enthusiastic Unitarian pastor, educated at Harvard University, arrived in Portland. The young reverend, Thomas Lamb Eliot, was a man of dreams.

He was also, though, a practical man, and soon his life's purpose was dedicated to improving his chosen city.

Reverend Eliot had a lofty aspiration: a Portland "enlightened"—a city moral and humane. His energetic labors quickly acquired for him the nickname "the conscience of Portland." He became the minister of one of the first churches on the West Coast. He founded the Oregon Humane Society—the fourth-oldest humane society in the nation. He championed the public library, public schools, and worked to improve the lives of the poor, orphans, and infirm. Yet, after toiling for thirty-five years, Eliot began fearing his hopes for his community were doomed to failure. All about him he saw the Portland he loved slipping in a direction to become, not progressive, but a crossroad of struggling humanity.

Never one to give up, however, Reverend Eliot decided to try a new tactic, an effort that over the years would prove more successful than he ever could have dreamed. He endeavored to set up a park system for Portland, and in 1899, under his persuasive insistence, the first Municipal Park Commission of Portland was formed by the Oregon Legislative Assembly.

Reverend Eliot was appointed to its first board of commissioners. Through his dogged persistence, he successfully advocated for the commission to contract the most important landscape architecture firm of its day, the Olmsted Brothers of Brookline, Massachusetts, to make a park-planning study for the city.

That one decision would markedly change the future of Portland.

In 1903, John C. Olmsted arrived and conducted thorough research of the city and its environs. Thoughtful, perceptive, and wise, he made several inventive, far-reaching suggestions. One novel idea was planning a circuit of connecting parks that looped around the city. Later, these would be known as Portland's famous "40 Mile Loop." Olmsted also proposed another visionary conception: that the hills west of the Willamette River, along the Tualatin Mountain Range, be acquired for an extensive park of wild woodland character.

"Rural parks are intended to afford to visitors that sort of mental refreshment and enjoyment which can only be derived from the quiet contemplation of natural scenery," Olmsted wrote. *"A visit to these woods would afford more pleasure and satisfaction than to a visit to any other sort of park. No use to which this tract of land could be put would begin to be as sensible as that of making it a public park."*

This proposal for such a native park was unlike any others the Olmsteds had ever conceived for an urban area. While there were numerous supporters, things didn't turn out as the Olmsted Brothers had intended. Rather, in 1907, when voters approved a million-dollar bond issue to carry out the Olmsted Plan, all the money went to developing existing parks, not to creating new ones. Again, in 1913, voters had another opportunity to preserve a significant part of the Tualatin Mountain Range. They voted it down.

In place of a park, however, eager land speculators laid out massive subdivisions all across miles of forested hills.

Change happened rapidly. Thousands of lots were platted alongside a network of imaginary roads. One of the most prominent realtors, Richard Shepard, planned an eleven-mile roadway that contoured in and out of the forested hillside's steep ravines to lure buyers into purchasing properties. In 1915, enlisting investors and engineers, Shepard built what today is known as Leif Erikson Drive, renamed in 1933 after the Viking explorer. Its $150,000 cost, however, was nearly twice as much as anyone had anticipated. To make matters worse, in its first year, a winter's landslide closed the road, and engineers estimated that it would cost an additional $3,000 to make repairs.

Shepard's dream soon became his worst nightmare. To cover costs for the road, the owners of the vacant lots were assessed. The vast majority, however, refused to pay. As a consequence, between 1915 and 1931, hundreds of lots, totaling 1,400 acres, were forfeited to the City of Portland for nonpayment of the assessment and taxes. In addition, other land along the Tualatin Mountain Range, after being logged off and subsequently burned by out-of-control slash fires, was forfeited to Multnomah County because of tax delinquency.

The idea to create the forest reserve that John C. Olmsted envisioned appeared to be forgotten. Fortunately for the growing city, a few advocates still held on to the hope that something could be done.

Three Portlanders believed in the Olmsted dream. Fred Cleator, regional forester for the US Forest Service and great lover of the outdoors known for his work in helping develop the Pacific Crest Trail, supported the idea of creating a "wilderness park for Portland." He was joined by Thornton Munger, a scientist recently retired from the position of chief of research for the Pacific Northwest Experiment Station. Garnett "Ding" Cannon, chairman of Standard Insurance Company and president of the Federation of Western Outdoor Clubs, was equally determined to create a new park for the city, what was growing in their minds as a "Forest Park."

Forty years after the Olmsted plan was written, the three individuals went to work. Cannon requested that the City Club of Portland conduct a study on the park's feasibility. Responding to his request, the City Club appointed a committee—John Carter, David Charlton, Allen Smith, Sinclair Wilson, and, as chairman, Cannon himself—to undertake the task. After two years, in August 1945, the committee published its findings in a report that strongly endorsed the idea of preserving the natural forest as a city park:

"Because of its rugged beauty and magnificent outlook . . . the committee is convinced that the area should be preserved for public forest-park use, and that such development should be of a primitive nature rather than as a park in the ordinary sense."

A month later, the City Club of Portland voted unanimously to support the creation of a 6,000-acre municipal forest park for the benefit of the community. Next, following the report's publication, the Portland City Planning Commission got involved. It recommended the creation of the "Forest Park," as proposed by the City Club.

From those green lights, Cannon began a program of action.

First, he began contacting multiple organizations and service clubs throughout Oregon to advocate for the park. Then, after campaigning for a year, Cannon called a public meeting of citizens, under the umbrella of the Federation of Western Outdoor Clubs, to come together for a remarkable goal. At this meeting, he met with astonishing success.

The "Committee of Fifty," a group of civic, commercial, educational, and recreational agencies, was formed. Working together, they would unite to formulate a plan to effectuate the proposed park. The organizations included:

Oregon Audubon Society
Oregon Federation of Garden Clubs
Portland Garden Club
Geological Society of the Oregon Country
Portland Council of Social Agencies
Federation of Western Outdoor Clubs
School District No. 1
Congress of Parents and Teachers
Catholic Youth Organization
Federation Jewish Societies
Portland Federation of Women's Organizations
Little Garden Club

Men's Garden Club
Oregon Roadside Council
Central Labor Council, AFL
Lions Club
4-H Clubs
The Pathfinders
Camp Fire Girls
Boy Scouts of America
Trails Club of Oregon
Izaak Walton League
Portland Chamber of Commerce
YWCA
Portland Industrial Union Council, CIO
Federated Community Clubs
Wayside Garden Club
Junior Chamber of Commerce
Portland Grade Teachers Association
Girl Scouts
East Side Commercial Club
Kiwanis Club
Multnomah Anglers and Hunters

Incredibly, many of these groups stayed closely affiliated with the Forest Park Committee of Fifty for decades, with changes only in the people representing the organizations over time.

After several meetings, the Committee of Fifty executed a petition. With Munger acting as chairman and Cannon as vice chairman, the petition was sent to the mayor of Portland and the city council. It requested that the city dedicate all city-owned lands in the area—including the 1,400 acres acquired by nonpayment of tax assessment (mostly the result of Shephard's folly)—for park purposes. It also asked that Multnomah County convey to the city all its delinquent tax-owned property, acquired after much of the property had been logged and burned, to become part of the park. Furthermore, it requested the City of Portland to adopt a policy of acquiring private lands within the 6,000-acre designated boundary of "The Forest Park."

On July 9, 1947, the Portland City Council was unanimous. It adopted the resolution. Following the decree, the City of Portland transferred 1,400 acres of land from the assessment collection division to the park bureau.

Ten months later Multnomah County, after overcoming several legislative obstacles, transferred 1,100 acres of land to the city park bureau without cost. In a marvelous gesture, School District No. 1, which would have received revenue if and when the tax-forfeited lands were sold, waived all claims, joining the others to create a park like no other.

A total of 4,200 acres of forest land was formally dedicated as *Forest Park* at a public ceremony on September 25, 1948. Commissioners from Multnomah County and the City of Portland acted as speakers. They were joined by members of the Committee of Fifty and a large audience. Reverend Charles Guilbert offered an invocation. Camp Fire Girls sang songs and Boy Scouts acted as color guards for the dedication. The joy was contagious. A vision proposed forty-five years earlier, which had looked impossible, at last became an actual and legal reality.

Today Forest Park spans 5,200 acres. While the Committee of Fifty has changed its name several times, in 1989 becoming the Friends of Forest Park, and in 2008, the Forest Park Conservancy, its mission and goals have stayed the same: to preserve, protect, and enhance this magnificent urban natural sanctuary for both people and wildlife. Working in tandem with Portland Parks and Recreation, the Forest Park Conservancy strives to provide safe and welcome access to all visiting the park. It has amassed over 2,000 volunteers who steward Forest Park and its trails. Beyond park borders, the conservancy has joined with partners to create the "Greater Forest Park Conservation Initiative"—a visionary roadmap to restore and protect not only the park but the surrounding forest ecosystem, which totals more than 15,000 acres.

For the last seventy-five years, thousands of citizens have come to cherish what Forest Park offers. With strong management and ordinances written to protect its unique qualities, it remains true to its original, visionary intention, thoughtfully stated by former Portland Parks director, Charles Jordan, in 1990:

"You will not find any place in America, an urban park, so close to the heart of a city, that provides the wilderness experience five minutes from downtown. Forest Park is unique. It is priceless."

Watersheds of Forest Park

> In the Pacific Northwest, rivers and the lands they drain provide a
> living link with our region's history and heritage. Watersheds have
> supported human life for millennia, and nurtured species such as
> salmon and Douglas-fir that are icons of our unique environment,
> people, and lifestyle. Their health preserves a legacy for future
> generations—the natural legacy on which our community originally
> was built and still defines who we are.
> —Portland Watershed Management Plan, 2005

Forest Park's predominantly undeveloped character plays an important role
within the city of Portland. Its vast unbroken area of forested land—spanning
eight miles from West Burnside Street to NW Newberry Road—functions as
a series of naturally occurring watersheds.

Eleven significant watersheds drain Forest Park and discharge clean,
cool water into the Willamette River and its tributary, Multnomah Channel.
Ranging from several hundred to over a thousand acres, these watersheds in
order of size include Balch Creek (1,550 acres), Doane Creek (1,037 acres),
Saltzman Creek (964 acres), Miller Creek (900 acres), Linnton Creek (855
acres), Springville Creek (695 acres), Newton Creek (447 acres), Johnson-
Nicolai Creek (389 acres), Alder Creek (340 acres), Thurman Creek (301
acres), and Willbridge (275 acres).

Assorted elements come together to create a watershed. More than just
a collection of random creeks between two banks, a watershed is a unifier. It
integrates the upstream lands it drains, the aquifers it recharges, and the lands
below that it inundates. Its waters are reflections of all the surfaces through
which they have flowed before ever reaching their banks.

Many factors influence a watershed's properties and together determine
its quality. Foremost among these are the size of the drainage, its geology,
topography, soils, vegetation, ecological functioning, and climate. Within
Forest Park drainages, geological features largely preordain observable
attributes. The entire park is stratigraphically uniform. It is underlain by a
lava bedrock—Columbia River Basalt—and topped by Portland Hills Silt,
wind-blown from the historic Columbia River floodplain. Because of this
geologic consistency, all watersheds within Forest Park have very similar

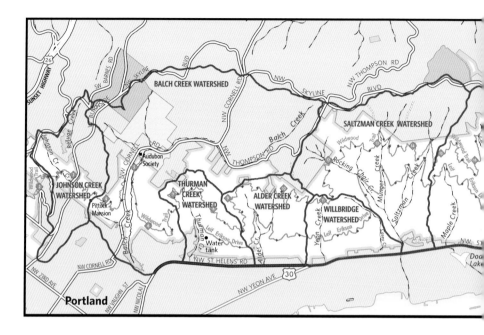

characteristics. This point is important, for variation among the watersheds is therefore attributable not to differences in geology but to differences in the activities occurring within individual drainages.

Learning to read the watersheds of Forest Park unveils the story of its natural and cultural history. Since the beginning, when the Tualatin Mountain Range became the dividing feature separating the Willamette and Tualatin River Basins, water has been the active sculptor creating the relief seen in the park today.

Over thousands of years, flowing water continually incised the thick silt layer beneath the park, stopping only when it reached the bedrock basalt. Ravine after ravine was formed as the streams discharged their burden and shaped and molded the many walls along the slopes of the mountain. The easily erodible nature of Portland Hills Silt, combined with the uplifting of the Tualatin Mountain Range, created a series of stream channels that are predominantly narrow and steep. On the average, the waterways of Forest Park exhibit a 15 percent slope, extending from the crest of Skyline Boulevard to the Willamette River 1,000 feet below.

The rapid vertical drop of this eastern slope has also resulted in creeks that are highly linear. In general, Forest Park creeks run directly downhill with little to no meandering. If not for the forest cover, the force and volume

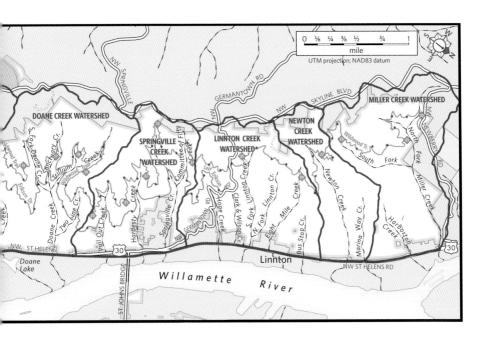

of the runoff from these streams could be considerable and damaging. Fortunately, the impact of precipitation is modulated by the heavily forested areas of Forest Park. Falling rain, which contributes to stream flow, is considerably slowed by its interception by the park's dense canopy of trees. When it at last reaches the ground, rainfall has lost much of its energy—power that could, if unabated, cause substantial erosion and downstream flooding.

The largely uninterrupted blanket of native vegetation of Forest Park, coupled with this high ecological functioning, are major factors contributing to the exceptional health of its watersheds. Much of the park's landscape is not damaged by fragmentation from development or intensive land use. Critical pieces of land, though, especially within some of the park's headwaters, are still privately held. If these areas are not protected and over time become developed, the future quality of the park's watersheds will be compromised.

Watershed headwaters are always essential areas. What happens in the headwaters affects everything downstream. For this reason, a watershed's headwaters require special attention and management. Upstream activities that upset natural hydrologic balance increase in magnitude as water moves downstream. In other words, downstream flooding, erosion, channel degradation, and transportation of pollutants all expand their capacities for damage if the native headwaters are degraded.

Fortunately, Forest Park's eleven major watersheds still predominantly function as they have for hundreds of years. Hydrologists studying Forest Park watersheds have determined they are the least altered watersheds within the City of Portland when compared with their historical conditions. Even more, two Forest Park streams—Miller Creek and Balch Creek—display attributes that are comparable to the best native streams across western Oregon.

At a time when urban ecosystems are particularly vulnerable because their resilience has been impacted by near-constant human disturbances, studies show that Forest Park watersheds are distinctly remarkable in giving us living models of healthy, urban streams.

The creeks of Forest Park, while predominantly acting in natural ways unobstructed by artificial features, face one significant barrier, however. As their flowing water prepares to leave the park to enter its large repository below, the Willamette River, streams are met with a major impediment—US Highway 30. At the abrupt intersection of streams with roads and industry, all natural water courses are disrupted. With the exception of only one waterway, Miller Creek, Forest Park native streams are captured into pipes and carried for considerable distances underground until they are at last discharged into the Willamette River. This separates the streams of Forest Park from the Willamette River, and, unfortunately, eliminates or reduces the diversity of fish communities in these otherwise high-quality habitats.

In essence, the healthy character of the watersheds of Forest Park is a visible manifestation of its history. A critical part of that narrative is the result of years of vision, research, planning, and ongoing management of the park. Securing the park's boundary conditions—from the Skyline crest to US Highway 30—continues to be of vital importance in preserving the soundness of its watersheds. This protection not only benefits the park's plants and animals and the deeply troubled Willamette River, it benefits all of us.

Vegetation of Forest Park

Inside the borders of Portland Oregon, there are more evergreens than in any other city on earth. Portland's boundaries enclose a wilderness. Every great city of America should have a museum of the America that was. Forest Park is such a museum. I truly hope there will always be men and women in Portland determined to keep it that way.
— Oregon senator Richard L. Neuberger, 1955

This will be a show place, unrivalled by any other city, to which to take visitors and introduce them to the lush forest flora of the Douglas-fir region.
— Thornton Munger, Forest Park Committee of Fifty, 1960

The adoption of preservation of natural systems is [Forest Park's] top priority.
— Forest Park Natural Resources Management Plan, 1995

Scientists agree that the forests of the Douglas-fir region of western Washington, western Oregon, and northern California are unique among all temperate forest regions in the world. A combination of factors, including the region's mild winters, historically dry and cool summers, the relative absence of hurricane-force storms, and the genetic potential of its tree species, make the area significant in three outstanding respects:

1. Species of coniferous trees of the region attain a greater age and size than those found anywhere else in the world.
2. In terms of the sheer plant material, these forests have a greater accumulation of biomass (living and decomposing vegetative matter) than any other of the earth's temperate forests.
3. In their native condition, Northwest forests are highly unusual in that they are dominated by coniferous trees.

In order to better understand the massive forests of the Pacific coast, scientists have subdivided the Douglas-fir region into specific areas that exhibit similar assemblages of plants and similar microclimates (rainfall and temperature). These vegetation zones are classified and named on the basis of an area's climax, or mature and self-perpetuating, vegetation. In western Oregon and Washington, the Western Hemlock Vegetation Zone encompasses the greatest area. Included within it is Portland's Forest Park. In its natural, undisturbed condition, this zone is forested primarily with three tree species: Douglas-fir, western hemlock, and western red cedar. To a lesser degree, grand fir, black cottonwood, red alder, bigleaf maple, madrone, and western yew trees also occur throughout the landscape. Shrubs of the zone are well developed. Common indicator species are sword fern, salal, Oregon grape, lady fern, red huckleberry, salmonberry, osoberry, and vine maple. The zone's predominant wildflowers include wild ginger, inside-out flower, Hooker's fairy bells, vanilla leaf, evergreen violet, waterleaf, and trillium.

Because Forest Park remains in a largely natural condition, it has maintained all of the Western Hemlock Vegetation Zone's naturally evolved, characteristic plants. However, one difference is significant today. Resulting from extensive logging in the past 170 years, a large portion of the zone, including Forest Park, is clothed with mosaics of red alder and bigleaf maple trees, instead of being dominated by evergreen trees. Under natural situations, red alder is abundant only in streamside areas of the Northwest.

What has caused the change? In areas that have experienced repeated disturbance to the natural vegetation, such as through intensive logging and brush fires, the soil becomes depleted of nutrients. Alder readily establishes itself under these conditions, sometimes choking out all the fir trees, unless the young evergreens have been seeded on the bare soil and gained a foothold concurrently with the encroaching alders. If Douglas-fir does not get going at the same time with young alder, it will not compete as well and may take a long time to grow into a stand and even then, only sporadically. Maples, too, can dominate locations that once were the realm of conifers if they successfully capture a site after initial logging has occurred and not relinquish it to firs.

Both hardwood species—bigleaf maple and red alder—have intriguing characteristics that play a role in their success after logging activity. Bigleaf maple trees actually favor mass soil movement and can thrive on relatively unstable ground and landslide deposits where other trees cannot.

Red alder—the most common hardwood in the Pacific Northwest—also benefits from disturbance and often increases in abundance after logging or burning. It has nitrogen-fixing nodules on its roots that increase nitrogen in the soil. In addition, alders have rapid juvenile growth, can tolerate poor drainage, and can easily eliminate Douglas-fir by invading disturbed areas and generating dense, young stands.

Conifers, in contrast, exhibit much slower juvenile growth when young. By about age forty-five, however, firs catch up. Beyond that age, Douglas-fir surpasses red alder in height. Over time, they will out-compete alders, as they can live hundreds of years, while alder is a relatively short-lived species with a maximum age of about one hundred years.

To explain the diversity of micro-habitats in Forest Park, it helps to understand how a Douglas-fir forest grows. As it ages, it goes through several observable changes. After a major disturbance such as fire, windstorms, logging, mudslides, or disease, a forest transforms and progresses along a relatively linear trajectory. If little disturbance affects it, it may reach, after 200 years, a climax stage. The series of conditions along the way are referred to as successional stages.

Approximately six successional stages can be observed in Forest Park. Because of differences in levels of disturbance, such as logging activities, forest fires, and tree plantings within the park, they are distributed as a mosaic throughout its 5,000 acres.

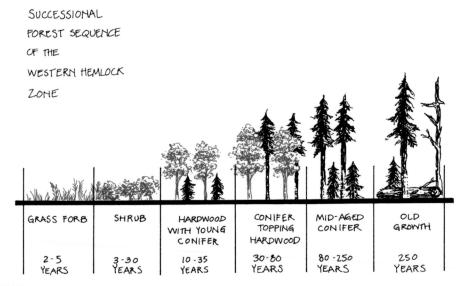

SUCCESSIONAL
FOREST SEQUENCE
OF THE
WESTERN HEMLOCK
ZONE

GRASS FORB	SHRUB	HARDWOOD WITH YOUNG CONIFER	CONIFER TOPPING HARDWOOD	MID-AGED CONIFER	OLD GROWTH
2-5 YEARS	3-30 YEARS	10-35 YEARS	30-80 YEARS	80-250 YEARS	250 YEARS

The first successional stage of a forest, occurring two to five years after the previous vegetation has been removed by logging, fire, or other major disturbances, is the grass-forb stage. This pioneering "forest" has a low profile—less than five feet tall—and contains no trees at all. Instead, it is identified by its numerous species of grasses and large patches of bracken fern, Canada thistle, and fireweed. In Forest Park, the grass-forb stage is rare in Forest Park, occurring mostly along the park's fire lanes and transmission powerlines.

When a forest is between three and thirty years old, after the initial disturbance, the shrub stage becomes apparent. Red alder, bigleaf maple, willow, and Douglas-fir trees begin to establish themselves at this time. But more noticeable, perhaps, is the variety of common shrubs that proliferate—thimbleberry, salmonberry, red-flowering currant, osoberry, and several species of blackberry—ranging in height from two to twenty feet.

The third successional stage observable in Forest Park is hardwood with young conifer. This becomes noticeable when a forest is between the ages of ten to thirty-five years, with the presence of young, thickly growing alder and maple trees, twenty-five to seventy-five feet tall, with girths of eight to ten inches.

If Douglas-firs have been able to get a start at the same time as the hardwoods, they will begin to "catch up" after forty years and exceed the deciduous trees in height. As the forest continues to grow, it enters the fourth successional stage—conifer-topping hardwood. This forest is between thirty and eighty years old, and apparent in many places in Forest Park.

Fifth in sequence is mid-aged conifer. This stage becomes noticeable when a forest has achieved the age of eighty years and is recognizable by stands of mature Douglas-fir trees. Because much of Forest Park was logged between 1913 and 1940, the mid-aged conifer stage covers large areas of the park. Red alder and bigleaf maple trees that live for only about one hundred years are growing old and dropping out of the vegetation scheme. Douglas-fir, which has a life span of more than 750 years, is still young and thriving and forming tall, stately stands. In Forest Park, numerous individual Douglas-fir trees, observable along many of the park's trails, are greater than one hundred years old, taller than 175 feet high, and larger than three feet in diameter at breast height.

In the shadows of these great trees grow a variety of younger, shade-tolerant conifers—western hemlock, western red cedar, and, on wetter sites, grand fir—where they can get a good start. The forest floor of this age class, too, is rich with plants. Sword fern, Oregon grape, red huckleberry, vine maple, and salal naturally flourish beneath the evergreens.

Finally, when a forest has escaped any major disruption for 175 years, the final or climax successional stage of vegetation becomes established. This is the old-growth stage. Patches of old-growth can be found along Balch Creek, in Springville and Newton Creek Canyons, and near Linnton Creek. Some younger stands in Forest Park also contain old-growth Douglas-firs—remnant trees that are greater than 200 years old and exceed six feet in diameter!

Old-growth areas are self-perpetuating and will continue indefinitely, unless something forces them back to an earlier condition. Past logging activities and substantial fires in Forest Park have dramatically reduced old-growth vegetation in Forest Park, yet its second-growth forests of mid-aged conifer are progressing to contain old-growth characteristics and display several indicative old-growth structural features.

Trees in the old-growth stage—predominantly western hemlock, western red cedar, and Douglas-fir—are observably old and huge. Douglas-fir stands, in particular, maintain their integrity for century after century. Of all conifers in the Western Hemlock Vegetation Zone—including western hemlock, grand fir, and Sitka spruce—Douglas-firs retain their intactness and biomass with reduced mortality and are less vulnerable to diseases and defoliating insects. Old-growth trees are often individualistic in appearance, many sporting broken-off crowns. Also present in these habitats is an abundance of large snags (standing dead trees) and dead and downed logs in various stages of decay. These last two features are also apparent in mid-aged conifer stands, but not in the quantity found in old-growth.

Far from being signposts of demise, decaying snags and downed logs in old forests help ensure that life-giving nutrients are being recycled back into the soil. Downed logs act as "nurse logs" for hemlock and Douglas-fir seedlings, which establish themselves on the nutrient-filled trunks. (Alder rots too fast to become a nurse log.) They are also very important for many species of wildlife, such as cavity-nesting birds and flying squirrels, which require them for breeding and feeding sites. In Oregon, woodpeckers are ten times more abundant in old-growth than in young forests. Amphibians and small mammals will use fallen trees for cover, refuge, breeding, and feeding. Many varieties of invertebrates, mosses, lichens, and fungi also favor old-growth habitats.

Research shows that old-growth areas play a critical function in the health of an ecosystem, for their giant trees hold within them rich gene pools containing characteristics such as longevity and the ability to ward off disease. They hold tightly to nutrients, such as nitrogen, that are often depleted in young stands. Taken together, all of the traits that characterize old-growth forests are vital for the welfare and stability of future generations of trees. Sadly, of all the age classes, old-growth forests are rapidly disappearing. This loss is substantial, because once gone, it requires over a century for forests to develop the structure and composition many species depend on. Even more, with climate change and hotter, drier summers in the Northwest, the scarcity of old-growth will make it difficult for forests to retain resiliency. Already scientists are finding that western hemlock trees, which are not tolerant of high moisture stress atmospheric conditions, are experiencing accelerated mortality. Hotter, drier summers could result in significant loss of western hemlock.

Fortunately, because of its tremendous value to future forests, to water-sheds, and to native species of wildlife, the park's mature, second-growth coniferous landscapes are being managed to naturally age and to develop climax attributes. Remarkable for a city of Portland's size, Forest Park today can be thought of as a living sanctuary for an evolving old-growth ecosystem.

Wildlife of Forest Park

> Forest Park supports a diversity of vertebrate wildlife that is dominated by birds. . . . In 1948, the year Forest Park was created, the Committee of Fifty declared that one of the five primary objectives for park creation was "to provide food, cover, and a sanctuary for wildlife." [Today] many of the park's birds are Special Status Species, and many bird species are in decline and species of concern. Perhaps no greater threat exists to the stated goal of growing an ancient forest and to the wildlife that would inhabit it than climate change.
> —John Deshler, *Forest Park Wildlife Report*, 2012

One hundred and five species of birds and sixty-two species of mammals can be observed living in or passing through Portland's Forest Park. This diversity of wildlife, the vast majority of which are species native to the Northwest, is highly unusual in comparison with parks in the nation's other major cities.

In most large metropolitan areas, urban development has resulted in a definite decline in the numbers of native birds and mammals. The usual progression of a city's expansion means that natural habitats disappear parcel by parcel, and that large, continuous natural areas are broken up by urban sprawl. Under these circumstances, native wildlife species are at a loss to respond. They become trapped within limited pockets of available habitat, cannot find mates with which to reproduce, and many species are unable to migrate to more hospitable natural areas, which are too far away. This concept is referred to by biologists as an "ecological sink" or "ecological trap."

What is the common result of urbanization? Many naturally occurring species fall prey to local extinction. Larger species that have more specialized requirements for breeding and feeding are often the first to disappear—the native hawks, owls, large woodpeckers, elk, bobcat, and deer. What remains is often non-native. Starlings, feral rock pigeons, Norway rats, and house mice proliferate in cities, these species finding no difficulty coexisting with humans. They readily immigrate from other urban areas as native species decline.

This is *not* the story of Forest Park.

Because of the park's exceptional size and, at present, the natural forest habitat of the Tualatin Mountain Range that connects with the Oregon Coast Range, large numbers of native birds and mammals live within Forest Park or migrate through it. Research conducted by the City of Portland to determine "Bird Integrity Index Scores" by measuring a variety of metrics—such as numbers of warblers, native cavity nesters, and neotropical migrants—found that Forest Park evinces the healthiest bird communities in the entire metro region. Even more remarkable, all species in Forest Park are native.

Similarly, two-thirds of the native mammal species known to reside in the Oregon Coast Range occur in Forest Park. Thirty mammalian species breed in Forest Park; nineteen species are abundant. Mammal diversity is dominated by small terrestrial rodents, predominantly deer mice, Douglas squirrels, and Townsend's chipmunks. Ten species of bats live in the park, as do coyotes, weasels, and bobcats. Among omnivores, Roosevelt elk and black-tailed deer both occur annually in the park, and deer are well distributed. Coastal (Pacific) giant salamanders are indicators of clean and cool rocky streams with adjacent mature forests, a combination not found in many other urban areas.

"Forest Park serves as a refuge for sensitive and declining birds in the city."

—David Helzer, terrestrial biologist, Bureau of Environmental Services, City of Portland

Research shows that Forest Park serves as a wildlife reserve for many forest interior species and provides important stopover habitat for numerous migratory birds. It is also a resource for many species now suffering decline. It has the highest number of at risk or Special Status Species in the region. These priority conservation species are determined by state and federal agencies, the National Audubon Society, Partners in Flight, and biodiversity centers.

Three dozen species, or one third of all Forest Park birds, are denoted as Special Status Species of concern. These include warblers, flycatchers, wrens, and woodpeckers. While many are abundant in Forest Park, they are nevertheless experiencing significant population declines in the region and some across all of Oregon. This reason alone makes Forest Park an important factor in working to preserve native wildlife. The park provides important habitat for breeding and nesting. It offers foraging habitat and an essential place for migrating avian species to stopover when hundreds or thousands of miles from their own breeding territories.

What is it that makes Forest Park such a sanctuary for wildlife? Three characteristics are noteworthy.

1. Forest Park's Mature, Structurally-Complex, Mixed-Conifer Forest Habitat
Animals respond to the structural components of vegetation. Because of this, the successional stages of a forest community can be thought of as different habitats for wildlife. Early successional stages of a forest, with their low-growing profile and open conditions, attract animals adapted to these particular conditions. Later successional stages, which have many layers of vegetation, snags, and downed logs, attract wildlife that require these components. For this reason, a person walking through low-elevation forests in western Oregon and Washington can expect to see different assemblages of birds and mammals, depending on which successional stage of the forest that person is in.

Much of Forest Park consists of mature, structurally complex mixed-forest stands. These tend to hold a greater abundance of key wildlife habitat components that are important to all wildlife classes. Large broken-top trees are especially valuable for many animals, particularly owls, bats, squirrels, and weasels that use them for breeding, nesting, feeding, and roosting. Large

logs are important for many amphibians and some reptiles because they provide hiding cover, retain moisture, and produce abundant invertebrates.

Five species of woodpeckers breed and are relatively abundant in Forest Park. Three—the pileated woodpecker, downy woodpecker, and northern flicker—are Special Status Species. Woodpeckers are especially dependent on snags and require them in varying stages of decay. They use snags with sound wood in which to excavate their nesting cavities. They need more deteriorated snags and logs in which to forage for insects. Woodpeckers are extremely important inhabitants in an ecosystem because many species of animals require holes in trees for nesting sites and do not have the ability to make them for themselves. For example, saw-whet owls, violet-green swallows, tree swallows, chestnut-backed chickadees, and red-breasted nuthatches, as well as Douglas squirrels and northern flying squirrels, are entirely dependent upon woodpeckers to drill holes in snags for them.

Among owls, five species breed in Forest Park. These include great horned owls, northern saw-whet owls, western screech owls, barred owls, and northern pygmy owls. Currently, the park is the premier research site for small, diurnal pygmy owls. This species shows remarkable breeding success in Forest Park, which is thought to be due to excellent breeding habitat and food resources. Its preferred diet consists of small mammals and birds and occasionally moths, and it favors live western red cedar trees for nesting, which are plentiful in Forest Park and offer an abundance of excavated cavities, thanks to the work of pileated woodpeckers.

Forest Park's remnants of old-growth specimens, and the structural component of its mature stands, contribute key wildlife habitat components and help account for its large bird and mammal numbers. This is in direct contrast to most city parks. In the majority of urban open spaces, features such as downed logs and snags are usually removed in an effort to create "park-like" settings. With these structures taken away, however, there are fewer places left for native wildlife to feed, nest, and breed. The diversity of birds and mammals, therefore, is sharply reduced.

2. Connection to the Coast Range via a Wildlife Corridor

Presently, Forest Park's northwestern terminus maintains a natural link that extends all the way to Oregon's rural Coast Range. Acting like a funnel, this forested connection along the Tualatin Mountain Range allows native animals to wander in and out of the park at will, thereby increasing the chances that local mammals and birds will be able to find suitable mates and appropriate habitat conditions and will not suffer genetic isolation and eventual extirpation. Mobility is crucial to survival for many animal species. Well-designed and functioning corridors can exert a pivotal role in maintaining ecosystem vitality.

3. Presence of Interior Forest Habitat

Interior forest habitat, defined as native woodland vegetation occurring in large, unbroken pieces and not dissected by roads, clear cuts, or residential or agricultural development, is becoming increasingly rare in urban areas. Yet many species of native mammals and birds, particularly migratory songbirds, are extremely dependent upon habitat that occurs deep within the forest, far from the "edge." Many animals that frequent edges of forests—such as European starlings, opossums, skunks, and raccoons—tend to be predacious or parasitic upon forest birds. This has wreaked havoc on native wildlife populations. Throughout the northeastern United States and southeastern coastal plains, for example, regional extinctions regularly occur as a result of loss and fragmentation of natural interior habitat.

Once more, Forest Park is set apart from other city parks in that it still retains a significant amount of exceptionally cohesive interior forest habitat north of Germantown Road. Because of its scarcity within urban areas, the worth of Forest Park's interior forest habitat only continues to rise. Those species determined to be most at risk are associated with this habitat type.

> **"Interior forest habitat is Forest Park's most unique and valuable asset. No other urban park in the United States offers anything comparable in quantity or quality."**
>
> —Forest Park Natural Resources Management Plan, 1995

Because of its naturalness and ecological functioning, Forest Park offers all who visit the opportunity to observe bald eagles and red-tailed hawks, nine species of colorful warblers, five species of industrious woodpeckers, and eleven types of singing wrens and sparrows. Hikers also have the chance to cross paths with coyotes, black-tailed deer, elk, and maybe even a bobcat.

What is outstanding is that all of these native Northwest species can be found in a metropolitan area of 2.5 million people, within the confines of one extraordinary city park.

Amphibians and Reptiles of Forest Park

Amphibians—a collection of fascinating species consisting of frogs, toads, and salamanders—have been part of our world for a long time. In fact, scientists believe amphibians were the first four-limbed animals to walk the earth. In the Pacific Northwest, thirty-two amphibian species occur in a wide range of habitats and within these various environments, they demonstrate distinct preferences during different stages of their development.

Forest Park is home to ten species of amphibians. These include six salamanders, one newt, which is a distinctive type of salamander, and three frogs. All the species that live in Forest Park, aside from the occasional, invasive bullfrog, are native, well-distributed, and abundant. Most amphibians will go unnoticed by visitors to Forest Park, however. They are small, elusive, and for the most part, silent. Yet within their home ranges, amphibians play a critical role in an ecosystem's food chain and nutrient cycle.

Amphibians provide an important source of food for birds, fish, and even some snakes. They consume numerous aquatic and terrestrial invertebrates. Moreover, they are intriguing creatures for several key reasons.

Amphibians and reptiles (collectively known as "herps") are cold-blooded vertebrates (animals with a backbone). They cannot control their body thermostat; their body temperature changes with their surroundings. Many amphibians start life in an aquatic form then transition to living on land. In this way, they are important in transporting nutrients from aquatic to terrestrial habitats. Curiously, amphibians are the only class of animals that does not have any special protective covering on their skin—no scales, feathers, or fur. Amphibians' skin is smooth, thin, and at real risk of drying out. This is one of the signature features that differentiates the class of amphibians from the class of reptiles. The skin of a reptile—snakes, turtles, and lizards—is thick and covered with scales. In contrast, amphibians' skin is "naked." For that reason, most amphibians live in moist, cool places.

One hundred years ago, when Portland was not as developed and much of its landscape was wetland and forest, amphibians likely ranged in greater numbers and locations. Since many wetland habitats globally have been filled in or paved over, amphibian populations have been declining worldwide. In an effort to understand what this means to ecosystem health, in 2008 scientists in Portland started surveying the city for amphibian abundance. This is valuable information as some amphibian species act as "canaries in the coal mine," being sensitive to negative environmental changes. If they start to disappear from watersheds, it is a signal that ecosystem health is declining and that other forms of native life are likely compromised.

Amphibians are equipped with numerous traits that adapt them for living in a variety of habitat types. Some salamander species are stream-loving, requiring moving water for breeding and egg-laying. Others need still or slow-moving water. Still other varieties are fully terrestrial, preferring moist, wet soil instead of pools of water. One limiting factor for species diversity in Forest Park is the scarcity of ponds and cold moving streams for species that need water for egg- laying. Some park streams, though, predominantly Balch Creek, Saltzman Creek, Linnton Creek, and Miller Creek, display great amphibian diversity.

Two species of stream-associated salamanders live in Forest Park. Pacific giant salamanders thrive in Balch Creek, as do Dunn's salamanders, which is a rare exception in Portland, as only a few other places in the city have reported them. This species lives on land as well as in water, lays their jelly-like eggs in moving streams, and produces young that have gills to breathe underwater! Some adults live in or under big logs in riparian forests. Others retain their gills and never metamorphose but become sexually mature in the larval form, remaining in the streams.

Two pond-breeding salamanders—long-toed salamanders and northwest salamanders—are also common, breeding at the Portland Audubon Society's pond that connects directly to the park and Balch Creek.

Terrestrial salamanders are fascinating animals, and two species are numerous throughout Forest Park. Ensatina salamanders, commonly known as "Oregon's salamander," and western red-backed salamanders are both fully terrestrial. They frequent the park in its moist, dark forest habitat where they lay their eggs underground or in rotting logs. Interestingly, these two species are known as "lungless salamanders" because they do not have lungs. Instead, they breathe through their skin! Smooth and thin, their skin acts as a respiratory surface where oxygen enters the body and carbon dioxide is released. Being so sensitive, it is not a good idea to pick them up if you see one by the trail. They are easily distressed, and their thin skin can be harmed by chemicals from warm hands.

Rough-skinned newts are another kind of salamander featuring webbed feet and a paddle-like tail. They also are locally plentiful in Forest Park but only at a few sites. Newts require cold, clean ponds for breeding. In the park, they are primarily found near Balch Creek because of its proximity to Portland Audubon Society's pond, where hundreds breed each year.

Two native frogs are also abundant in Forest Park. Because of their small size and quiet behavior, however, they are usually unseen by hikers. Pacific treefrogs reside throughout Forest Park in moist upland and riparian habitats. Occasionally, if a person is lucky enough to be at the right place at twilight during the frog's breeding season (January–March), they can hear the upwelling vocalizations of Pacific treefrogs, also known as Pacific chorus frogs, singing the song of spring.

Northern red-legged frogs also occur in Forest Park, which is known to host the largest population of the species within the city of Portland. Northern red-legged frogs are listed as an Oregon vulnerable species and a federal species of concern. While currently numerous in Forest Park, these frogs face a serious problem. They require wetlands to breed and lay their eggs. For those individuals in the northern part of Forest Park, the lack of ponds and wetlands means they must face the perilous journey from the security of the park to wetlands which lay across a major thoroughfare—US Highway 30. What results is hundreds being killed by fast moving cars every year.

But that is changing. For the last eight years, an annual volunteer effort, called the "Harborton Frog Shuttle" has come to help the frogs make the crossing. Approximately one hundred "frog taxi volunteers" commit to an entire season to spend wet, cold nights picking up migrating frogs. Carefully placing them in specialized buckets, they ferry them in vehicles across the highway and release them to the desired wetlands. After egg-laying season ends, these volunteers help the frogs safely make the reverse trip back to the forest.

Each year over 2,000 frogs have been saved by the efforts of these stalwart volunteers with the assistance of Oregon Department of Fish and Wildlife, Oregon Department of Transportation, West Multnomah Soil and Water Conservation District, Portland Parks and Recreation, and Multnomah County. Eventually, volunteers hope to find a longer-term solution to the problem. Partnering with Portland Parks and Recreation, they are working to identify safe breeding habitat within the park and to possibly create new ponds so frogs won't be required to cross the deadly road. Other individuals are investigating the possibility of constructing one or more underpasses for the frogs to use.

Reptiles are another group of residents of Forest Park, though species numbers are few. Turtles do not occur at all in Forest Park, as the habitat does not favor them. Turtles need sunny permanent ponds with adjacent uplands, a feature Forest Park lacks. Only two reptilian species—the common garter snake and northwestern garter snake—are spotted regularly in the park and both are well distributed. They can be seen in summer along open, sunny utility corridors and fire lanes. There have also been reports of western fence lizards, western skinks, and northern alligator lizards in the dry, open upland parts of Forest Park. Unlike thin-skinned amphibians, reptiles have evolved to live on dry land, are protected by scales, and breathe through lungs, not gills or skin.

Forest Park supports a surprisingly high number of species of amphibians and reptiles in the city and acts as a vital sanctuary for common and more rare species. With increased understanding, it is hoped that the conservation of native herps will continue, and their great significance to healthy ecosystems become more widely recognized and valued.

Pollinators of Forest Park

Pollinators are important contributors to the Forest Park ecosystem. The open environment under the park's powerline corridors provides necessary habitat and acts as a sanctuary for these essential animals. To appreciate the tremendous value of pollinators, however, it helps to understand the role they play in our environment and how they function in Forest Park.

The research is clear: pollinators are indispensable to our lives. In fact, one in three bites of food that we eat comes from the work of pollinators. Furthermore, 85 percent of flowering plant species depend on insects, birds, and other animals to transport pollen. In addition, 75 percent of all global food crop types benefit from animal pollination.

Pollen is essential to ecosystem health, but what is it exactly, and what do pollinators do? Pollen is a plant's male sex cells. These must be transferred to the stigma—the female part of a flower—of the same plant or another flower, for the plant to produce fruit and seed. While some plants are self-pollinated, plants like wildflowers cannot transport pollen without the assistance from a pollinator.

Many animals visit flowers to help provide this service, such as bees, butterflies, moths, birds, beetles, flies, and wasps. Of them all, though, bees are the most effective pollinators as they are the most efficient at transporting pollen. Their bodies have evolved to be very capable at carrying large amounts. Both male and female bees visit flowers to feed on nectar and females deliberately gather pollen to bring back to their nests for the young. The hairiness of some bees also makes them highly productive pollinators. Male bees are often observed covered in pollen, even though they are not intentionally gathering it for their offspring.

Approximately 4,000 species of native bees can be found in North America, with an estimated 630 species of bees native to Oregon. While hiking in Forest Park under transmission corridors, keep an eye open for bumble bees, the park's biggest and most conspicuous bees. Unfortunately, here and throughout the world, pollinators are experiencing declines. This is especially true among many species of wild pollinators and creates a serious problem for the ecosystem services needed for animal-pollinated plants, including crops.

What does this mean, economically speaking? In the United States alone, the value of crop pollination is between $18 and $27 billion annually. Worldwide, the economic value of insect pollination is estimated between $235 and $577 billion annually. The continued loss of pollinators could produce severe impacts.

Three of the greatest threats to native pollinators are habitat loss, fragmentation, and pesticide use. Specific to Oregon, prairie areas, which are important environments for pollinators, are also diminishing. Recognizing these significant declines in both species and critical habitat, researchers have made Forest Park's open corridor habitat under power transmission lines the sites of pioneering new studies. The methods they have formulated are collaborative, innovative, and wonderfully creative.

Two major energy companies—Bonneville Power Administration (BPA) and Portland General Electric (PGE)—have constructed powerlines that run through Forest Park. Interestingly, these corridors afford some of the only open habitat in Forest Park and are important for offering resources pollinators can forage. At several locations in the park, a hiker will see signposts stating, "This area has been planted with native flowering plants to provide habitat for butterflies, bees, birds and other pollinators." This is the result of a state-of-the-art partnership that began in 2016 between the Xerces Society, Metro, Portland Parks and Recreation, and BPA. Working together, these groups have a shared commitment to both improve habitat and collect data on pollinators in Forest Park.

Named the "Pollinator Powerline Project," this innovative endeavor includes close monitoring of pollinators, including bees and butterflies, and their responses to active restoration of habitat in BPA corridors. Early results of these studies are showing that the removal of invasive vegetation, at the same time restoring these habitats with native willows, shrubs, and wildflowers, is benefitting pollinators.

Scientists know that the majority of animal pollinators need a diversity of flowers in order to survive. At the same time, most plants require a diversity of pollinators. In the second year after intensive planting of flowers and shrubs, investigators found that native plant species were increasingly visited and attracting more pollinators in the restored corridor.

Bee groups found residing in the park include bumble bees, honey bees (not native to the Northwest), mason bees, sweat bees, mining bees,

and long-horned bees. Among butterflies, painted ladies, Lorquin's admirals, western tiger swallowtails, California tortoiseshells, whites, sulphurs, blues, and grass skippers are also observed in Forest Park.

The results from these Forest Park studies are significant. They highlight an exciting new opportunity for conservation management of pollinators. Managing powerline corridors to provide safe transmission of electricity *and* restore habitat by planting mosaics of native floral resources has the potential to dramatically benefit wild pollinators. As these studies continue, it is hoped that their results will encourage further endeavors and collaborations between power companies and conservation groups for the benefit of increasing populations of vital species.

Pollinators are a prerequisite to the integrity of biodiversity, to global food webs, and to human health. When walking through Forest Park, be on the lookout for bees and butterflies. Spying one, consider for a moment what this means: you are standing in a place where pollinators are beginning to thrive with the help of scientists and volunteers restoring populations of these critical partners to our life on earth.

Lichens of Forest Park

Have you ever wondered about the inconspicuous gray or green leafy or tufted strands that grow on or along the limbs and trunks of trees? Or the crusty splotches of gray, green, black, or orange often seen on rock outcrops and the trunks of some trees, like red alder? These unique forms are known as lichens, which are a special collaboration of two or more different organisms that function together as a single structure called a lichen. Lichens represent some of the earliest forms of life on earth. The oldest fossil evidence dates them back at least 400 million years, and there are over 100,000 known lichen species.

What are lichens exactly? Are they a plant or a moss? Actually, they are neither. Because lichens are a composite form containing a variable mixture of fungi, algae, cyanobacteria, bacteria, and archaea interacting with each other, it has been difficult for scientists to classify them. Presently, lichens are categorized with the kingdom fungi and by their fungal component. Yes, they are grouped together with mushrooms, but they aren't the mushrooms we commonly think of!

Lichen composition is unique. The photosynthetic partner of the lichen—alga or cyanobacteria—produces food for the fungus, converting atmospheric carbon dioxide into carbohydrates. The fungal partner forms a physical structure for the alga—providing a surface to capture moisture and minerals and a structural "home." The nature of this collaboration of partners allows lichens to live in a variety of habitats where neither partner could survive by itself. In addition, cyanobacteria, which are microorganisms related to bacteria, are not only capable of photosynthesis but have the additional capacity to "fix," or convert, nitrogen from the air into a form of nitrogen that plants can use for growth, providing an essential process which is very important in our otherwise nitrogen-limited Pacific Northwest forests. Nitrogen is important because it is a major component of chlorophyll and also amino acids, the building blocks of proteins.

Remarkable to comprehend, the structure of lichens is formed through the *interactive effects* of each of the organisms involved. The result is the creation of a whole much greater than the sum of the parts—something that none of the partners can do without the others. In other words, the balance that has emerged is a *cooperative relationship* that has allowed all partners to thrive in ways they could not do alone. Scientists today consider the complex nature of lichens to reflect a self-sustaining ecosystem!

Because of our moist, temperate climate, lichens play a large role in the Forest Park ecosystem. Those growing on rocks are the first colonizers of these surfaces—the pioneers. They slowly dissolve the underlying rock, releasing minerals, and forming a veneer of soil for mosses and other plants to gain a foothold and a place for them to begin to grow.

In forests at mid to high elevation, lichens that have the ability to fix nitrogen are the major source of this important nutrient to other forest members. Those species with cyanobacteria can break the bond in nitrogen in the air and make it usable for plants that need nitrogen but can't derive it from the air themselves. As the lichens drop to the ground after storms or when tree limbs fall, they break down and release their nitrogen to the soil, like a fertilizer for others to use.

Lichens provide plentiful benefits in other ways as well. During the winter when other food resources are scarce, they are a major food source for a number of animals. Also, numerous species of birds use lichens to build into their nests. Further, lichens are also an invaluable indicator of air quality. Because those lichens found in trees depend on the surrounding air to get the water and minerals they need, they also can accumulate air pollutants (heavy metals and macronutrients). When air pollution is too high for them to manage, they will die. The distribution of various lichen types and chemical analysis of them is a standard method to assess air quality all over the world.

Lichens can be easily observed in Forest Park, especially in fall and winter after significant rain and storm events. Those that have been blown down from the tree canopy can be found all along the forest floor and trails throughout the park. One of the most easily identified is *Usnea*, a genus whose members have gray, thready strands forming a covering on branches. Another, less common variety, *Lobaria pulmonaria*, or "lungwort," is commonly described as "lettuce growing in the trees." This species, in particular, is sensitive to air pollution, and its presence or absence is widely used as an indicator of air quality. Interestingly, in the 1970s, a survey of Forest Park did not find it in the area, suggesting it was either absent or quite rare. With steps taken to improve air quality in the intervening years, including removal of lead from gasoline,

Lobaria pulmonaria is making a slow comeback. For several years, *Lobaria* has been spotted with increasing frequency in Forest Park.

The importance of competition as a force in nature has been heavily emphasized in our culture since Darwin's writing in the nineteenth century. As evidenced by the relationships seen between lichens and the greater forest community, however, cooperation and collaboration are no less important in shaping our world. Stop to pick up a fallen fragment of a lichen on the trail and realize you are holding a collaboration of very different organisms in your hand, a cogent reminder that everything in the forest is connected.

Fungi of Forest Park

When people think of fungi what often comes first to mind is the gray fuzzy growth appearing on old bread or stale food, or, in the forest setting, the occasional mushroom. What many of us don't realize is that the vast majority of fungal species exist completely out of sight. There are millions of types of fungi in the world, many found in places you would never guess—in mid-ocean vents, rocks, and throughout our GI tract!

When we observe a mushroom or crust, we are actually seeing a short-lived, fruiting body of a fungus. This is only a tiny portion of the underlying fungus, however. Some varieties permeate the ground and connect many types of trees and understory plants while others penetrate wood and plant debris. Beneath the ground is a great network of fungal threads that connects to trees and other plants that provide them minerals and water from the soil. It also allows them to trade nutrients, water, and the minerals they need to grow.

In essence, fungi are unseen community collaborators and community recyclers. Under the surface, fungal threads envelop and fuse with tree roots and link nearly every tree in a forest. They play a very important role in a forest, such as Forest Park, forming life-giving partnerships.

Neither plant nor animal nor bacteria, fungi belong to their own kingdom: Fungi. They are thought to have evolved in the oceans 1.2 billion years ago from a single-celled organism with a small tail (flagellum). Humans appear to share this same common ancestor, making fungi more closely related to us than to plants. Also like human beings, fungi can't make their own food—as plants can—and so are dependent on external sources for their nutrition.

In the forest setting, there are two basic ways they do this. One group has developed special enzymes that allow them to obtain nutrients by breaking down woody material left behind when a tree or plant dies. They can also potentially get nutrients from leaves, duff, dung, bones, and even feathers. Fungal cells form thin, long threads and net-like structures (mycelium) that proliferate and can completely permeate the underlying material such as a dead tree or debris. From this process, they obtain the sugars necessary for their nutrition and return the remnants to the soil to be used again by living plants. The mushrooms, crusts, and shelf mushrooms we see on the surface of dead trees produce spores that can travel widely and start the process all over again in another site in the forest.

A second group of fungi have developed a means of collaborating with surrounding trees and plants to form a symbiotic, mutually advantageous relationship from which they get their nutrition. These varieties generally do not grow on dead trees or plant debris. Rather, they form a vast network underground! Fungal threads attach to the *roots* of different trees and plants, and spread widely throughout the surrounding soil, penetrating down all the way to the underlying rock. From this attachment, fungi receive the sugars they need for nutrition. In exchange for this benefit, they also aid the forest in six vital ways:

- The fungal network, called mycorrhiza, tremendously expands the collective root zone of trees and plants . . . up to forty times! This magnified collective root capacity allows trees and plants to find deep water sources in dry weather.

- The network enables plants to access minerals that the fungi can uptake from water in the soil or dissolve from underlying rock.

- Chemical messages can be transmitted throughout the system, which facilitates a form of communication and resource allocation to take place between individuals—think of it as a social network. Scientists have found that large, older giants of trees—termed "Mother Trees"— are able to sustain their seedlings and other forest-floor plants directly by providing sugars for their nutrition through this powerful web.

- Mycorrhizal fungi can also sequester heavy metals, thereby protecting plants in the network from the toxic effect of these elements.

- In some cases, mycorrhizal fungi create structures that host nitrogen-fixing bacteria and supply trees with this essential nutrient.

- Some types of saprophytic fungi are first to colonize an area after a fire, acting like "first responders." A consequence of forest fires is the formation of a dense layer of organic material under the surface, sometimes down a foot or more, that hinders the ability of water to penetrate the soil. This makes it difficult for plants to recolonize. Fungi play an important role in breaking down this layer so that the cycle of plant growth can come back to a burned area.

When are fungi most likely to be encountered in Forest Park? Although they can be observed year-round, the fruiting bodies of forest fungi are easily spotted in spring or fall. Keep a lookout for mushrooms, brackets, crusts and jellies on logs, trees, and the forest floor during these seasons. All of these are varieties of fungi.

Two common species frequently noticed in the park are the western grisette (*Amanita pachycolea*) and the artist's conk (*Ganoderma applanatum*). Grisettes are examples of a mycorrhizal fungus and are associated with the surrounding trees. Artist's conks get their nutrition from breaking down wood. Interestingly, the artist's conk continues to grow for multiple seasons as long as there is underlying wood to use and forms rings on the bracket's surface pores each year. By counting its rings you can establish its age!

While largely unseen, the complex interrelationships that exist between forest fungi and neighboring plants and animals form a tightly knit and interdependent community, of which we, too, are a member. Fungi are truly the forest's decomposers, recyclers, and essential partners in a powerfully important alliance. Without the cooperation of fungi and plants, the forest as we know it would not be possible. And a great place to study them? The sanctuary of Forest Park.

Mosses of Forest Park

An iconic feature of northwestern forests and, in particular, Forest Park, is how verdant the woods become in fall with the return of rain. Myriad hues of vibrant green light up the landscape from late autumn through spring. Branches of bigleaf and vine maple trees, adorned with plush mosses, undergo transformation when wet. Mosses reawaken in the fall from their summer dormancy, festooning the forest throughout the winter and into spring as long as rain continues. Forming green leafy tufts or mats, they live on the limbs and trunks of trees, on old rotting logs or rocks, and on patches of bare earth in spots with sufficient moisture.

Mosses are plants. But what interesting plants they are! They were a very early development in plant evolution, dating back 400 million years ago, and their unique characteristics have allowed them to thrive ever since. They are generally small—from a half inch to four inches. They do not have flowers; they do not have seeds. Even more intriguing, they do not have true roots. They function by absorbing water and necessary nutrients through their leaves, which are only one cell thick over much of their surface.

Mosses retain an intimate contact with the surfaces upon which they grow. If dry weather is sustained, they have the remarkable ability to merely dry up and remain dormant until moisture returns, at which point they promptly return to active growth. Their suite of unique traits allows them to grow in niches within the forest where other vascular plants—land plants with tissues for conducting water and minerals throughout the organism—cannot. It is estimated there are about 12,000 species of moss on earth and numerous varieties in Forest Park.

Different kinds of mosses are associated with certain forest features. For example, in Forest Park, magnificent moss (*Plagiomnium venustum*) is frequently seen growing around the base of bigleaf maple trees. It forms a cluster of bright green tufts around the aboveground portion of the tree's roots. Oregon beaked moss, another feather-like species, is a common ground cover in wet areas of the forest floor, and drapes over the branches of many trees you pass on Wildwood Trail.

Mosses contribute greatly to the overall health of the forest ecosystem. Their ability to hold large quantities of water permits rain to drip slowly into the underlying ground, being cooled and purified in the process, and maintain moisture levels for other forest inhabitants. Healthy watersheds depend on this attribute. As well, because of their capacity to become dormant when sparse soils dry out and their ability to absorb nutrients directly through their surfaces, mosses can begin to colonize rock surfaces where lichens have begun to create soil. In time, this process creates habitat for other vascular plants to live.

Some species of moss can form symbiotic, or mutually beneficial, relationships with nitrogen-fixing bacteria. Nitrogen-fixing bacteria are organisms that can transform nitrogen from the air into compounds useable by plants. This allows barren soils to become capable of supporting the growth of other plants. Colonization also happens along tree branches of deciduous trees, when mosses create a "canopy soil" that provides a home for countless insects and other creatures. Birds in particular are able to find a food source in habitats where mosses proliferate in winter.

The wealth of their unusual qualities has made mosses useful to mankind for thousands of years. Archeologists discovered that the "Iceman" found in northern Italy, over 5,000 years old, had both lichens and mosses in his pouch! Because of their great water-absorbing ability and antiseptic characteristics, Indigenous people have long used mosses in diapers and as a material to

bind wounds. Mosses have been crafted to make baskets, ropes, medicines, and to treat injuries as well as used for insulation and sealants in traditional log houses. Similar to lichens, mosses are also often used as environmental-monitoring systems. They directly absorb water and minerals from the air and adjacent soil and are an important indicator of air quality.

As you hike the trails of Forest Park in different seasons, look for mosses along the way and observe what a stunning transformation occurs as the yearly cycle unfolds.

Trails of Forest Park

Forest Park represents an unparalleled resource, where citizens can enjoy the peace, solitude, ruggedness, variety, beauty, unpredictability and unspoiled naturalness of an urban wilderness.

—Forest Park Natural Resources Management Plan, 1995

Introduction to Forest Park Trails

A visit to Forest Park is a time for discovery and inspiration. With eighty miles of trails to explore in a park that is not only beautiful but also acts as a biodiversity reserve, it provides a woodland experience rarely available to people inhabiting a major city. Forest Park is a haven for families, hikers, bird-watchers, nature photographers, runners, cyclists, equestrians, scientists, teachers, and students—in short, anyone seeking close-in natural refreshment, wellness, and joy.

Two major routes transverse much of the length of the park. Wildwood Trail, at 30.1 miles, is a designated National Recreation Trail. It spans Forest Park end to end—from downtown Portland to NW Newberry Road—and is the longest natural woodland trail winding through a city park anywhere in the United States. Many of the hikes outlined in this book include segments of Wildwood Trail; it also is a great experience to do in its entirety.

Leif Erikson Drive is another long park pathway. Its 11.2 miles are closed to all motorized vehicles, and it is popular among hikers, equestrians, and cyclists. Leif Erickson Drive traverses many of the park's watersheds and intersects with numerous interesting perpendicular trails that can be used for making a variety of loop trips.

To help with your exploration, *Forest Park* presents twenty-one enjoyable hikes, covering a total of seventy-five miles, and featuring the majority of the park's trails. These are tailored to different experiences and to what one might be looking for on a given day, and a given season.

▬	Hikes 1–10	**Great Hikes for Families and Kids**
▬	Hikes 11, 12	**Great Hikes for Wildflowers**
▬	Hikes 13, 14	**Great Hikes for Birdwatching**
▬	Hikes 15–17	**Great Hikes to Get to Know Your Ecosystem**
	Hike 15	**Understanding Watersheds**
	Hike 16	**Understanding Wildlife Corridors**
	Hike 17	**Understanding Interior Forest Habitats**
▬	Hikes 18–21	**Great Hikes for Getting in Shape**

To aid navigation, each hike has updated, color maps and elevation profiles. Descriptions of all trails with wayfinding information are included. In addition, there are discovery elements to deepen interest as you explore. "Did You Know?" and "Can You Find?" are exciting ways to learn more about your forest and ecosystem as you head out on the trails!

While visiting Forest Park, I encourage you to take some mindful minutes to linger and consider what surrounds you. Open up all your senses: What spots of loveliness can you see? What sounds can you hear? The wind? A singing bird? A chittering Douglas squirrel? What don't you hear? (Consider: sounds of the city.) Touch the bark of an old-growth tree and reflect again how old it is, how much history it has seen. Smell the healthful, invigorating scents of the fir trees. Take a moment for a *sanctuary pause*. These are times of observation and reflection that can provide inspiration and peace. I note in the hikes descriptions places that have especially touched me with their grandeur and beauty. You will find many more!

There are a few guidelines to be aware of to keep your Forest Park trip safe and enjoyable. To maintain the park's wilderness character, be sure that anything you bring in you also carry out. There is no camping or fishing allowed in the park. Harvesting or picking of plants is not permitted. (An important exception to this rule is removing invasive English ivy.) Fires are strictly prohibited. Off-leash dogs are a serious problem in Forest Park and can be devastating to native wildlife. Dogs must be kept on a leash and remember to clean up all dog waste and pack it out. All trails, roads, and fire lanes in Forest Park are open to pedestrians. Designated trails are also open for cyclists and equestrians. Permitted trail uses are noted at trailheads and for each hike in this book. With the exception of official vehicles, motorized vehicles are not allowed anywhere in the park.

Forest Park is considered the nation's preeminent city park for its sheer immensity (5,200 acres), the diversity of its vegetation and wildlife (over 100 species of native birds and more than 50 species of mammals), and the vibrant health of its ecosystem. I hope you will get to know it and to appreciate it. Get involved with the Forest Park Conservancy and their many volunteer opportunities, from repairing trails, becoming a docent and crew leader, and removing invasive plants. Take time to create your own hikes of discovery.

Together, let us work to protect and preserve this outstanding urban sanctuary and keep Forest Park a welcome and safe place for all who enter.

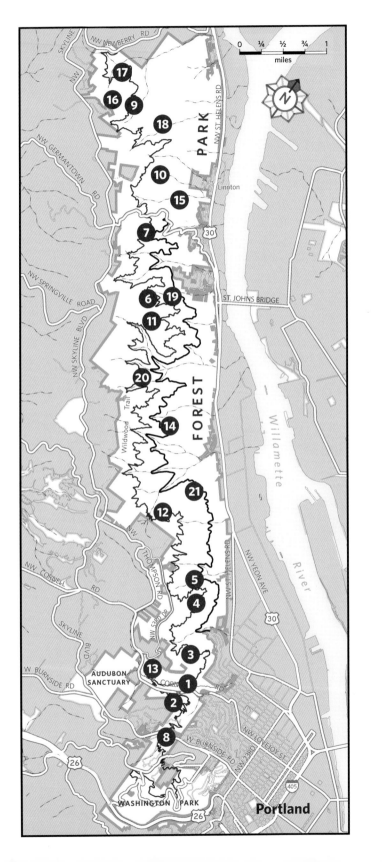

Directions to Trailheads

Lower Macleay Park Trailhead
From downtown Portland, travel north on NW 23rd Avenue until reaching NW Thurman Street. Turn left on Thurman. After five blocks, Thurman intersects with NW 28th Avenue. Turn right on 28th Avenue and continue for one block to NW Upshur. Turn left on Upshur and stay on the street (crossing 29th at the stop sign) until Upshur dead ends at the Lower Macleay Park headquarters.

Macleay Park/NW Cornell Road Trailhead
Travel west on NW Cornell Road 1.7 miles from the intersection of NW 23rd and NW Lovejoy (Lovejoy becomes Cornell Road beyond NW 25th). Look for a large stone monument honoring Donald Macleay alongside Cornell Road. Beyond the rock wall is a turnoff to the right where there is ample parking.

Holman Lane/Birch Trail Trailhead
Travel west on NW Cornell Road 2.2 miles from the intersection of NW 23rd and NW Lovejoy (Lovejoy becomes Cornell Road beyond NW 25th). At the intersection of Cornell with NW 53rd Drive, turn right on 53rd and continue for 0.5 miles. A parking area is on the left, across the road from a sign that says Birch Trail. To reach Holman Lane and the beginning of the trail, walk down 53rd Drive 200 yards to an unmarked gravel road. Turn left onto the road, which is a public right of way, and hike 0.06 mile to a locked park gate that demarcates Holman Lane.

Wild Cherry/ Dogwood Trailheads
Travel on NW Lovejoy Street from NW 23rd Avenue (Lovejoy becomes NW Cornell Road just after NW 25th) and drive 2.2 miles. Turn right on NW 53rd Drive and continue for 0.9 miles to a large parking area along the side of the road.

Alternatively, travel northwest along NW Skyline Boulevard. After crossing the intersection of Skyline Boulevard and NW Cornell Road, continue northwest for one mile to NW Thompson Road. Turn right on Thompson and travel for 0.5 miles until reaching NW 53rd Drive. Turn left on NW 53rd Drive and continue for 0.9 miles to reach the ample parking area.

Springville Road Trailhead
Travel west from NW 23rd Avenue and NW Lovejoy, which will become NW Cornell Road, and travel 3.3 miles to the junction with NW Skyline Boulevard. At the intersection of Cornell Road and Skyline, turn right onto Skyline and travel 3.8 miles to NW Springville Road. Turn right (east) on Springville Road and continue for 0.1 miles to a large parking area.

Alternatively, travel northwest along NW Skyline Boulevard. After crossing the intersection of Skyline Boulevard and NW Cornell Road, continue 3.8 miles farther on Skyline to reach NW Springville Road. Turn right on Springville Road and continue for 0.1 miles to the parking area.

Germantown Road/Leif Erikson Trailhead
Travel northwest on US Highway 30 (NW Yeon Avenue) 5.8 miles from the intersection of US 30 West and Interstate 405. Continue past the St. Johns Bridge and turn left at the traffic light immediately after the bridge. This is NW Bridge Avenue and the northern ramp to the bridge. Take the first right onto NW Germantown Road and follow it for 1.3 miles to a large parking area on the left, which marks the end of Leif Erikson Drive.

Alternatively, travel northwest along NW Skyline Boulevard. After crossing the intersection of Skyline Boulevard and NW Cornell Road, continue 4.7 miles farther on Skyline until its intersection with NW Germantown Road. Turn right on Germantown Road and continue for 0.8 miles until reaching the Leif Erikson Parking Area on the right.

Hoyt Arboretum
From downtown Portland, travel west on US Highway 26. Take the Oregon Zoo exit and continue past the zoo on SW Knights Boulevard. At Knights' intersection with SW Fairview Boulevard, turn right and go 220 yards farther to the Arboretum visitor's center. Hoyt Arboretum can also be reached by Max Line Rail to the Washington Park Station, or by TriMet bus, which stops in front of the visitor's center.

BPA Road/NW Skyline Boulevard Trailhead

Travel northwest along NW Skyline Boulevard. After crossing the intersection of Skyline Boulevard and NW Cornell Road, continue 5.7 miles farther on Skyline. The parking area can accommodate up to six cars. It is somewhat difficult to see as it is off the road and near a row of mailboxes with numbers beginning at 9640. The start of the hike, BPA Road, is well marked on a large, green park gate.

Newton Road/NW Skyline Boulevard Trailhead

Travel northwest along NW Skyline Boulevard. After crossing the intersection of Skyline Boulevard and NW Cornell Road, continue 5.1 miles farther on Skyline to reach NW Newton Road. Turn right on Newton Road and continue for 0.3 miles where the road ends at a parking area.

Upper Firelane 1 Trailhead

Travel northwest along NW Skyline Boulevard. After crossing the intersection of Skyline Boulevard and NW Cornell Road, continue on Skyline for 1 mile to the intersection with NW Thompson Road, coming in on the right. Turn right onto Thompson Road and travel 0.5 miles until the intersection of NW 53rd Drive, coming in on the left. Turn onto NW 53rd Drive. Travel 0.1 miles to the intersection with NW Forest Lane, marked with a sign. Turn left on NW Forest Lane (which is actually the beginning of Firelane 1) and continue for 0.3 miles, until it meets a locked park gate. At this point, hike 0.4 miles to the trailhead.

Portland Audubon Society

Portland Audubon is located at 5151 NW Cornell Road. Parking is available.

Lower Saltzman Road Trailhead

Travel northwest on US Highway 30 (NW Yeon Avenue) 3.7 miles from the intersection of US 30 West and Interstate 405. Look for NW Saltzman Road on the left. Turn left onto Saltzman and drive the paved, winding road 0.7 miles to a locked park gate. Parking is available along the road.

Linnton Trailhead

Travel northwest on US Highway 30 (NW Yeon Avenue) 6.6 miles from the intersection of US 30 West and Interstate 405 until reaching the town of

Linnton. The trailhead, marked by a large sign, is on the west side of NW 105th, and parking is available.

Firelane 15 Trailhead

Travel northwest along NW Skyline Boulevard 6.2 miles from the intersection of Skyline Boulevard and NW Cornell Road. Parking is available alongside Skyline Boulevard on a limited basis. The entrance to Firelane 15 is identifiable by a park gate on the east side of Skyline Boulevard beneath two major transmission lines that pass over the road at this point.

Newberry Road Trailhead

From downtown Portland, travel northwest on US Highway 30 (NW Yeon Avenue) 8.5 miles from the intersection of US 30 West and Interstate 405. Turn left onto Newberry Road and travel 1.5 miles. Wildwood Trail, marked by a sign, is on the left side of the road. Limited space is available for parking alongside Newberry Road.

Alternatively, travel northwest along NW Skyline Boulevard. After crossing the intersection of Skyline Boulevard and NW Cornell Road, continue 7.3 miles farther on Skyline to reach NW Newberry Road. Turn right onto NW Newberry and continue for 0.5 miles to reach a limited shoulder parking area on the right, adjacent to Wildwood Trail.

Lower Ridge Trail Trailhead

Parking is difficult. Currently, there is limited parking on the south ramp of the St. Johns Bridge. Plans are in discussion to renovate parking here. In the meantime, to reach the trailhead which is near the top of the ramp, a good idea is to take public transportation. Better yet, park in St. Johns and walk across the beautiful St. Johns Bridge to access the steep staircase that leads to the trailhead of Ridge Trail.

Upper Saltzman Road Trailhead

Travel west from NW 23rd Avenue and NW Lovejoy (Lovejoy turns into NW Cornell Road after NW 25th) for 3.3 miles to the junction with NW Skyline Boulevard. Turn right onto Skyline and proceed 2.9 miles to NW Saltzman Road. Turn right and continue 0.1 miles farther to reach the Saltzman Parking Area.

Alternatively, travel northwest along NW Skyline Boulevard. After crossing the intersection of Skyline Boulevard and NW Cornell Road, continue

2.9 miles farther on Skyline to reach NW Salzman Road. Turn right on Saltzman Road and continue 0.1 miles to the parking area.

Lower Firelane 1 Trailhead

A large, thirty-space parking lot, newly constructed by Portland Parks and Recreation, is located at 4315 NW St. Helens Road, at the three-way intersection of NW St. Helens Road, NW Yeon Avenue, and NW Kittridge Avenues. From here the trailhead begins. The area is easily accessible by TriMet bus from downtown.

Great Hikes
for Families and Kids

HIKE 1
Lower Macleay Trail, Stone House, and Wildwood Trail

DISTANCE: 3 miles
HIKING TIME: 1.5 hours
DIFFICULTY RATING: Easy
WATERSHED: Balch Creek Watershed
TRAILHEAD: Lower Macleay Park

Foot traffic only.

MILEAGE AND DIRECTIONS
0.0   Begin at Lower Macleay Park Trailhead at NW Upshur.
0.9   Arrive Stone House. Lower Macleay ends. Continue straight on Wildwood Trail.
1.4   Junction with Cornell Road and Portland Audubon Society. Turn around and descend.
3.0   End at Lower Macleay Park Trailhead.

One of the most scenic trails in Forest Park, Lower Macleay Trail is a magnificent introduction to the natural beauty of the park. It boasts rushing streams and giant primordial trees and is easily accessible by car or bus. The trail is a good example of the Pacific Northwest's Western Hemlock Vegetation Zone, considered by scientists as unique among all temperate forests in the world. In addition, the hike offers a chance to experience the richness of the Balch Creek Watershed. Balch Creek and its encompassing 1,550-acre watershed, with much of its natural qualities exceptionally intact, is considered one of the highest valued resource areas in the city of Portland.

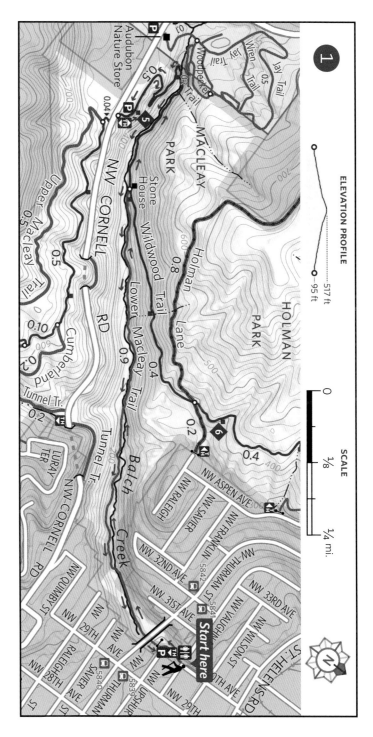

DID YOU KNOW?
The Sad Tale of Danford Balch

Balch Creek is named after infamous Danford Balch, who in 1850 staked out a 640-acre land claim in the hills west of town near the stream. Nine years later, Danford gained fame as the first Oregonian to be convicted of murder and hung in Oregon, after having shot his son-in-law to death. Questions, though, always remain if it were an "accident" or not? Danford always proclaimed his innocence. Before his execution, he divided his land claim in half—half for his wife and half for his nine children. Danford's dying statement was that proceeds from the sale of his lands would allow his children to be educated.

Unfortunately, that never came to pass. Danford's widow remarried a man widely regarded to be a lout. The Balch children were appointed a "guardian," swindled out of their inheritance, and never received an education. In 1886, the *Oregonian* recorded that through "villainous fraud, minor children were despoiled of their inheritance and turned out upon the world without education or property."

DID YOU KNOW?
A Member of the Salmon Family Lives in Balch Creek!

Closely related to steelhead, rainbow trout, and Pacific salmon, native cutthroat trout—a species of the family Salmonidae—have a healthy population in Balch Creek. Between 2,000 and 4,000 trout, ranging in size from 1 to 8.5 inches in length, live in this stream. Landlocked because they can no longer migrate to and from the Willamette River after the Lower Macleay Park pipe was installed, this isolated population remains viable and vigorous. (Just remember, no fishing allowed!)

CAN YOU FIND?

A Witch's Castle

The old Stone House, often referred to as the "Witch's Castle," is a significant piece of architecture built on the banks of Balch Creek. Designed in 1929 by architect Ernest F. Tucker, it was constructed to be a picturesque picnic shelter and public restroom for early visitors to Macleay Park. Architect Marvin Witt proclaims, "Observing the meticulous way in which the stones are fitted, no one who studies this ruin can doubt that the workmanship was of the highest caliber. Once upon a time, the old Stone House was the handsomest comfort station in the land."

DID YOU KNOW?

Forest Park Is An Educational Gold Mine!

If you learn the birds, plants, lichens, fungi, pollinators, amphibians, and mammals of Forest Park, you can go to any native forest in western Oregon and Washington and be familiar with the regional ecology! Teachers throughout Portland bring students of all ages to study the rich biodiversity of this amazing natural sanctuary.

BEGIN THE HIKE at the entrance to Lower Macleay Trail, located in Macleay Park.

Macleay Park was named for Donald Macleay, banker and civic leader, who in 1887 donated 105 acres of land to the City of Portland for a park. The land still retains the same name although it has been incorporated into Forest Park when the park was created in 1948. The hike begins as a paved path that passes under the Thurman Street Bridge and follows alongside Balch Creek. At the start, the stream can be seen dropping approximately forty feet to enter a concrete culvert where it flows underground for 1.25 miles to an outfall on the Willamette River. For a quarter mile, Lower Macleay Trail is a handicapped-accessible trail, and presently the only ADA trail in the park. More are anticipated, as the Forest Park Management Plan stresses that creating more trails for disabled visitors is "high priority."

Balch Creek is a 3.5-mile-long perennial stream and Forest Park's largest creek. Historically, the waterway was thought to support a variety of native fishes. Species diversity decreased significantly, however, after lower Balch Creek was diverted into a pipe in 1921; fish could no longer migrate to and from the Willamette River. Yet the stream still maintains a vigorous population of resident cutthroat trout, estimated between 2,000 and 4,000 individuals. Scientists have documented that Balch Creek's cutthroat communities are the healthiest in the entire city of Portland.

Continue on Lower Macleay Trail as it gently winds up Balch Creek Canyon, passing by massive Douglas-fir trees. At almost a mile, the trail ends at a well-marked junction with Wildwood Trail, Milepost 5½. Here you will find the remains of an unusual stone structure that stands prominently and is fun to explore.

Continue hiking upstream on Wildwood Trail as it follows Balch Creek. After crossing a footbridge at Milepost 5¼, the trail gains elevation as it switchbacks up to NW Cornell Road. At Milepost 5, Wildwood Trail intersects Cornell Road, located at a parking area. Adjacent is a picnic area with tables. Located 300 yards west of this spot is the headquarters of the Portland Audubon Society. A trip to its nature center, bookstore, and adjoining three wildlife sanctuaries is highly recommended. (See Hike 13.) To finish the hike, turn around here, retrace your steps, and return to Lower Macleay Trailhead.

HIKE 2
Upper Macleay Trail to Pittock Mansion Loop

DISTANCE: 2.2 miles
HIKING TIME: 1.5 hours
DIFFICULTY RATING: Easy
WATERSHED: Balch Creek Watershed
TRAILHEAD: Macleay Park/Cornell Road

Foot traffic only.

MILEAGE AND DIRECTIONS
0.0   Begin at Wildwood Trail at Cornell Road. At 0.04 mile, turn right on Upper Macleay Trail. Hike Upper Macleay Trail.
0.6   At junction of Upper Macleay with Wildwood, turn right on Wildwood Trail. Hike 0.4 miles.
1.0   Arrive Pittock Mansion. Explore, turn around. Go back down Wildwood. Continue for 1.4 miles.
2.2   Wildwood Trail ends at Cornell Road.

This easy, family hike offers vistas of beautiful Balch Creek Canyon and Watershed. It leads to Pittock Mansion, a Portland historic landmark originally built in 1914 by Henry L. Pittock, founder of the *Oregonian*. The Pittock Mansion today is fully restored, open to the public, and administered by Portland Parks and Recreation. Balch Creek, tucked far below in the canyon, is remarkable for its high resource values and ecological significance. It provides a living model of healthy urban streams. Balch Creek, in Forest Park's South Unit, and Miller Creek, located in the park's North Unit, have the richest aquatic insect communities in the city of Portland, which is a primary indicator of watershed health.

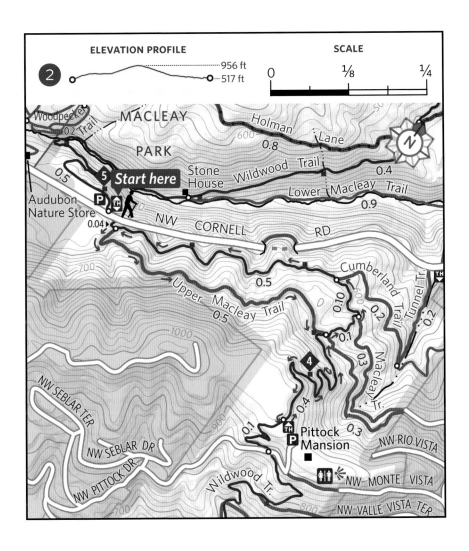

ELEVATION PROFILE

956 ft
517 ft

SCALE

0   1/8   1/4

DID YOU KNOW?

A Historic Mansion, Set for Demolition, Was Saved by Swift Community Action!

Pittock Mansion, a 16,000-square-foot mansion built in 1914 as a private home for the Henry Pittock family, featured luxuries few homes knew at the time. Designed by architect Edward Foulkes, it had forty-four rooms, an elevator, a central vacuum system, and interiors decorated in a diverse collection of styles. Henry, an avid outdoorsman, mountaineer, and publisher of the *Oregonian*, and his wife, Georgiana, were able to enjoy it for only five years, however. Henry tragically died in 1919 from influenza. The mansion stayed in the family for forty years, but fell into disrepair, suffering extensive damage during the Columbus Day Storm of 1962. The family considered tearing it down. Fortunately, the specter of demolition of a valued historic resource roused a community. Within three months, citizens raised $75,000. In 1964, the City of Portland, recognizing such strong community support, purchased the entire estate including forty-six acres for $225,000. Today Pittock Mansion is fully restored. The Pittock Mansion Society, in collaboration with Portland Parks and Recreation, operates and preserves the historic buildings and museum and offers tours of twenty-three of its rooms.

DID YOU KNOW?

Who Uses Those Holes in the Dead Trees?

Woodpeckers excavate nesting cavities in snags, but they aren't the only ones who use them to live in. Many species of birds and mammals do

not have the ability to make the holes themselves and depend on the work of the woodpeckers. Without them, they wouldn't have a place to nest! Northern pygmy owls and Douglas squirrels, for example, are entirely dependent on woodpeckers—nature's housing contractors—to drill holes in snags for them!

DID YOU KNOW?

What Bird, Once on the Brink of Extinction, Now Has Ten Nests in Forest Park?

The bald eagle, the United States national emblem! In the twentieth century, with numbers plummeting due to prior use of the pesticide DDT, the species was close to disappearing in the contiguous United States. In 1973 the regal bird was put on the endangered species list, and DDT was banned by federal action. Through strong conservation efforts, the species was rescued, and populations slowly recovered. Today, bald eagles call Forest Park home, and there is even a nest along this trail!

BEGIN THE HIKE heading south on Wildwood Trail at its trailhead on NW Cornell Road. After one hundred yards, Wildwood Trail intersects Upper Macleay Trail. Turn right onto Upper Macleay Trail and follow it as it parallels Cornell Road and Wildwood Trail from above. Through the tall trees, fine views of the Balch Creek ravine can be seen across the road. The complete watershed covers 2,248 acres (approximately 3.5 square miles), of which 1,500 acres are protected in Forest Park.

After a half mile, Upper Macleay Trail ends at an intersection with Wildwood Trail. Turn right onto Wildwood and head uphill. A half mile farther, at the crest of the hill, Pittock Mansion becomes visible. A visit to this historic museum and forty-six-acre scenic grounds and formal gardens is well worth it.

To return, descend for one mile on Wildwood Trail. Beyond Milepost 4¼, indicated by a blue diamond on a tree, Wildwood intersects Upper Macleay Trail. Proceed on Wildwood, following several switchbacks. Pass Macleay Trail, coming in from the right and a little farther, pass Cumberland Trail. Stay on Wildwood Trail and continue descending the canyon until NW Cornell Road and the trailhead. Along this lower section, try to identify the native shrubbery of the Western Hemlock Vegetation Zone. Oregon grape, sword fern, and salal grow abundantly on hillsides dominated by Douglas-fir.

HIKE 3
Holman Lane, Wildwood Trail, and Birch Trail Loop

DISTANCE: 2.6 miles
HIKING TIME: 1.5 hours
DIFFICULTY RATING: Easy
WATERSHED: Balch Creek Watershed
TRAILHEAD: Holman Lane

Foot traffic only on Wildwood and Birch Trails. Holman Lane allows bicycles traveling uphill only.

MILEAGE AND DIRECTIONS
0.0   Begin at Holman Lane at its intersection with NW 53rd Drive.
0.8   Turn left at the junction with Wildwood Trail.
2.3   Turn left onto Birch Trail.
2.5   Intersection with NW 53rd Drive.
2.6   End at NW 53rd Drive Trailhead.

This short, easy loop gives a taste of wild Northwest areas and fine examples of native plants and animals, all within a ten-minute drive from the city. Holman Lane was named for Frederick, Mary and George Holman, children of a pioneering family who donated fifty-two acres to the city for a park in 1939. Frederick, an avid rose exhibitor, remains distinguished in Portland's history as the person who gave Portland the name "City of Roses."

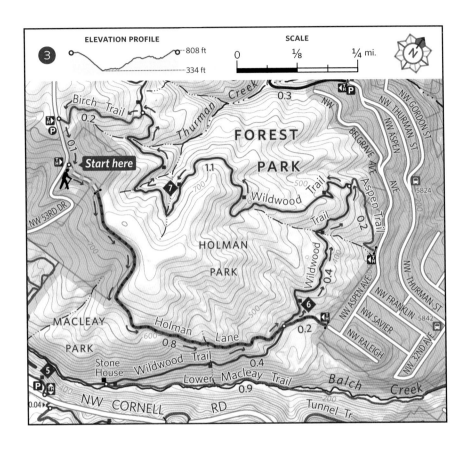

DID YOU KNOW?

If Frederick Holman Had Gotten His First Choice, Holman Park Would Now Be Holman Suburb

In 1910, Frederick Holman proposed to turn his land into a large development of residential homesites. He called it "Mountain View Estates." The *Oregonian*, in enthusiastic support, ran an article and a rendering of this plan under a prominent headline: "How to Beautify a Hillside." Landslides, however, crushed this dream before it even began. Thirty years later, Holman and his family donated their fifty-two-acre forested property to become parkland and connect with Macleay Park, which many considered a much better idea!

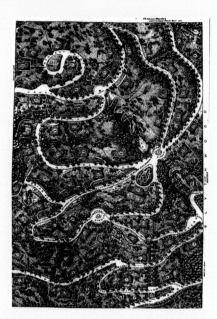

DID YOU KNOW?

The Greatest Mimic in Forest Park

One of the most common birds in Forest Park is the native Steller's jay—the West Coast's cousin of the blue jay. Steller's jays hold a strong resemblance to blue jays but sport a distinctive contrast: they have a black back and black head topped with a high black crest. Their call—a raucous "shaak, shaak"—can be heard echoing from

high in the firs throughout the park. Yet many times this forest mimic prefers to pretend it is a different bird altogether, emitting calls sounding just like a red-tailed hawk, and fooling even the best bird-watchers!

DID YOU KNOW?

What Fungi, Named for a Shellfish, Benefits Forest Park?

Oyster mushrooms (*Pleurotus* sp.) can be found in Forest Park and are often seen growing on decaying hardwood trees, like this red alder on Holman Lane. Yet rather than hurting the tree, which is dying from other causes, they enrich the forest by helping to decompose the dead wood and return essential elements and minerals to the ecosystem to be used by other plants and organisms.

CAN YOU FIND?

Ivy League? Not Forest Park!

Forest Park is proud to be a member of the "No Ivy League!" Started by volunteer Sandra Diedrich, the alliance to defeat ivy has grown and now includes the Forest Park Conservancy, Bureau of Environmental Services, Portland Parks and Recreation, and numerous volunteers—all working together to control the noxious spread of English ivy in Forest Park. This invasive plant is highly detrimental and threatens to choke out and take over the natural habitat of the park. The spread of English ivy is one of the greatest threats to plant and wildlife diversity and abundance in the park.

TO REACH THE TRAILHEAD from the Birch Trail Parking Area, walk down 53rd Drive 200 yards to an unmarked gravel road. Turn left, and hike to a locked park gate that demarcates Holman Lane. Go around the gate to access the lane, which soon becomes a grassy, wide pathway with a peaceful ambiance. For three-quarters of a mile, it gradually descends into the Balch Creek Canyon. Beautiful groves of mature coniferous trees adorn the hillside to the north. When the leaves are off the deciduous trees in fall and winter, views of Macleay Park, the Balch Creek ravine, and NW Cornell Road (across the canyon) can be seen to the south.

Holman Lane intersects Wildwood Trail just before Wildwood Milepost 6. Turn left (north) on Wildwood and hike for 1.5 miles. Throughout this portion of trail, native plants characteristic of western Oregon can be seen. Try to identify these signature plant and shrub species of the Douglas-fir ecosystem: osoberry, sword fern, red huckleberry, and waterleaf. Invasive species are also observable here and are in some places prominent—primarily English ivy. For thirty years, volunteer groups such as the No Ivy League and the Forest Park Conservancy have cooperatively worked with Portland Parks and Recreation in a tenacious, ongoing battle to eliminate and stop the spread of ivy and other destructive invasive species. Their hard work pays off: where the ivy has been removed, seed beds of vanilla leaf, Oregon oxalis, salal, maidenhair fern, and other native plants are given a chance to emerge and grow, regaining their rightful place in the ecosystem.

After Milepost 6¼, Aspen Trail joins Wildwood to the right. Continue on Wildwood and follow several switchbacks that gradually rise several hundred feet as the trail climbs up the ravine. Between Mileposts 6½ and 7, Wildwood Trail winds through another beautiful stand of straight, tall firs. Just before Milepost 7½, Birch Trail intersects Wildwood. Turn left onto Birch Trail and ascend through stands of red alder and bigleaf maple. Birch Trail comes out at NW 53rd Drive, concluding the loop.

HIKE 4
Wild Cherry Trail, Wildwood Trail, and Leif Erikson Drive Loop

DISTANCE: 2.7 miles
HIKING TIME: 1.5 hours
DIFFICULTY RATING: Moderate
WATERSHED: Thurman Creek Watershed
TRAILHEAD: Wild Cherry/Dogwood Trail

Foot traffic only on Wild Cherry, Dogwood, and Wildwood Trails. Leif Erickson Drive also allows bicycles and horses.

MILEAGE AND DIRECTIONS
0.0   Begin at Wild Cherry Trailhead on NW 53rd Drive. Hike Wild Cherry Trail.
0.3   Turn left onto Wildwood Trail.
0.9   Intersect with Dogwood Trail. Turn right and descend on Dogwood Trail.
1.2   Intersect with Leif Erikson Drive. Turn right onto Leif Erikson.
1.8   Turn right onto Wild Cherry Trail.
2.7   Arrive at Wild Cherry Trailhead.

For an easily accessible, short walk, this loop is one of the nicest in Forest Park. These trails, especially great for younger children, provide an excellent introduction to the joys of hiking. Everyone will appreciate its more open woods, where native shrubs and wildflowers can be readily observed. Not far from the center of the city, these trails yet impart quiet, naturalness, and beauty. Here, the bustling urban area seems to fade away.

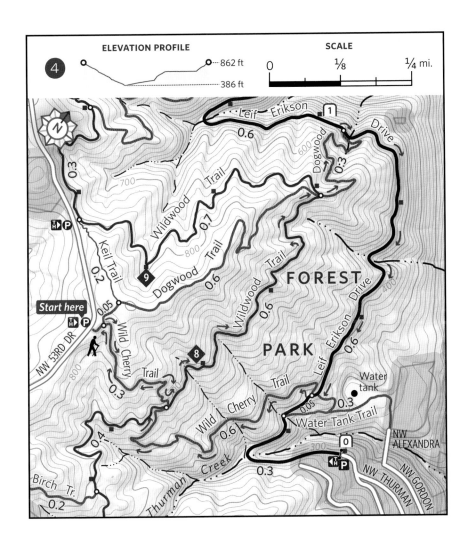

ELEVATION PROFILE

4 ⎯⎯ 862 ft
⎯⎯ 386 ft

SCALE

0   ⅛   ¼ mi.

N

Leif Erikson 1
0.6
Drive
600
Dogwood
0.3
0.3
700
Wildwood Trail
0.7
H P
800
Keil Trail
0.2
Dogwood Trail
0.6
9
0.05
Wildwood Trail
0.6
FOREST
Start here
H P
0.6
Leif Erikson Drive
400
Wild Cherry
0.3
Trail
8
PARK
0.6
Water tank
NW 53RD DR
800
Wild Cherry
Trail
0.05
0.3
0.4
0.6
Water Tank Trail
0
NW ALEXANDRA
Birch Tr.
Thurman
Creek
0.3
H P
NW THURMAN
NW GORDON
0.2
300

CAN YOU FIND?

Evidence Where a Wildcat Land Promoter Washed Out Thousands of Cubic Yards of Earth in Forest Park in Hopes to Fill in a Lake

(Hint: Look at a Ditch Next to Wildwood Trail near Milepost 8.)

In 1906, Lafe Pence had a mountain-moving idea: to wash soil off Tualatin Mountain and fill in Guilds Lake, far below, to create prime industrial development land to subdivide. Even though illegal, before anyone could stop him, Pence constructed fourteen miles of wooden flumes and sluiced 200,000 cubic yards of earth from hundreds of streams that percolate on the hillsides. Part of the project went straight through Macleay Park. His venture was finally halted by L. L. Hawkins, city park commissioner. Without Hawkins's intervention, Macleay Park would have been ruined, and Forest Park would look vastly different today.

CAN YOU FIND?

A Forest Park Marker Used for Map-Making Across the World

Look closely along lower Dogwood Trail near its junction with Leif Erikson Drive. Affixed to the ground, you will spy a round brass disk, called a US Coast and Geodetic Survey marker. These "benchmarks" were placed as part of triangulation surveys. Land surveyors used them to establish angles and distances between points. The placement of these tablets

was originally mandated in 1807 to survey lands along the coastlines and to act as markers delineating key reference points on the earth's surface. Today, the National Geodetic Survey's database contains data on over 1.5 million points that have helped measure and map the world.

CAN YOU FIND?

A Cone that Looks Like Little Mice Are Hiding in It

While hiking along Forest Park trails, be sure to look down. Scattered beneath the trees are assemblages of interesting cones that have dropped from the many trees growing in the forest. The Douglas-fir's cone, found everywhere in the park, comes with a story.

A Pacific Northwest Indigenous legend tells that once there was a sweeping fire in the forest. Fearing for their lives, all the animals tried escaping, but the small mice could not outrun it quickly enough. They begged different trees for help, but the trees could not provide shelter. At last they came upon a giant Douglas-fir tree, who told the mice to run up its bark and hide in its fir cones. The mice and the tree survived. Today, if we look closely enough, we can still see little hind feet and tails of the mice sticking out from the scales of Douglas-fir cones!

BEGIN THE TRIP at the Wild Cherry Trailhead and hike until its intersection with Wildwood Trail. The trees along the trail are predominantly red alder and bigleaf maple intermixed with many second-growth Douglas-firs, some reaching very large and impressive proportions. Native plants grow thickly in the understory, and varieties of sparrows, wrens, nuthatches, kinglets, and other native songbirds can be heard calling from the woods as one follows the pleasing footpath. At the intersection, turn left on Wildwood Trail and hike for a half mile.

Along this section of Wildwood Trail, between mileposts 7¼ and 8¼, keep a lookout for a depression, or ditch, on the left, upper side of Wildwood. Now overgrown and hardly visible, over a century ago this had been built as a flume by a land speculator named Lafe Pence. His plan was to sluice water from the north canyon wall and carry the spoils of soil to fill in Guilds Lake. His scheme ended with bank failure, to the great relief of many park advocates.

At the intersection of Dogwood Trail, turn right onto Dogwood. After a quarter mile, Dogwood ends at Leif Erikson Drive. Turn right onto Leif Erikson and hike along the wide, level, paved road, which is closed to all motorized vehicles except those on official park business. Views of the Willamette River, the city of Portland, and snow-capped mountains are visible through the trees. After a half mile, Wild Cherry comes in at the right. Turn onto Wild Cherry Trail and continue uphill for a mile along the scenic pathway to return to the trailhead.

HIKE 5
Dogwood Trail, Leif Erikson Drive, Alder Trail, Keil Trail,
and Wildwood Trail Loop

DISTANCE: 3 miles
HIKING TIME: 1.5 hours
DIFFICULTY RATING: Moderate
WATERSHED: Thurman Creek Watershed; Alder Creek Watershed
TRAILHEAD: Wild Cherry/Dogwood Trail

Foot traffic only on Dogwood, Alder, Keil, and Wildwood Trails. Leif
Erikson Drive also allows bicycles and horses.

MILEAGE AND DIRECTIONS
0.0 Begin at Dogwood Trail Trailhead at NW 53rd Drive. Hike Dogwood
     Trail.
0.7 Cross Wildwood Trail. Continue on Dogwood.
1.0 Turn left on Leif Erikson Drive.
1.6 Turn left on Alder Trail.
2.5 Turn left on Wildwood Trail.
2.8 Turn right on Keil Trail.
3.0 Turn right on Dogwood/Wild Cherry Trail junction.
3.1 End at NW 53rd Drive.

This relatively easy loop close to town is perfect for an early morning walk on a
sunny day. In fall, the trails are especially scenic, owing to the predominance
of deciduous trees with their colorful, changing leaves. For most of its way,
the well-maintained route weaves through open groves of maple and alder,
interspersed with vigorous, tall Douglas-firs and bounteous native ferns. The
more open sections provide a chance to observe a chattering Douglas squirrel
or a busy Townsend's chipmunk. The peaceful sight and sound of perennial
Alder Creek is an ample reward for this short loop hike.

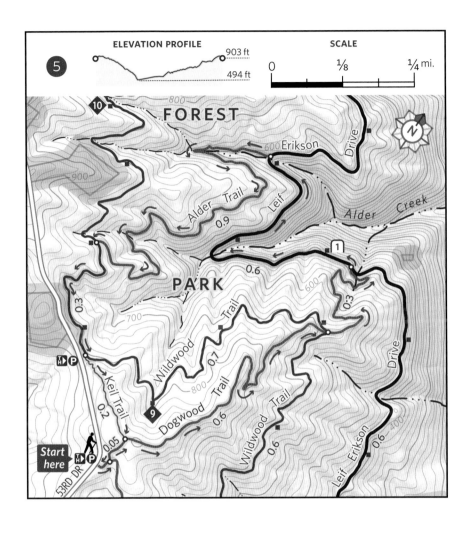

ELEVATION PROFILE

903 ft

494 ft

SCALE

0   ⅛   ¼ mi.

FOREST

Erikson

Drive

Alder Creek

Alder Trail
0.9

Leif

1

0.6

0.3

PARK

600

700

0.3

Wildwood Trail
0.7

800

Keil Trail
0.2

9

Dogwood Trail
0.6

Wildwood Trail
0.6

Leif Erikson Drive
0.6

400

0.05

Start here

53RD DR

CAN YOU FIND?
The Four Fabulous Ferns of Forest Park

Sword Fern

Keep your eyes peeled for a luxurious fern that grows in abundance in the park. You'll know it because its leaves resemble a short, broad sword. It remains green all year long and is hard to miss because it commonly grows up to four feet high. This is a fern of the deep forest of the Northwest. It loves the  shade of dense stands of firs and hemlock in the Oregon Coast Range and grows in glades in Forest Park.

Maidenhair Fern

When is a fern unlike any others? When it is a maidenhair. This low-growing, delicate fern loves the rich, moist forests of the Northwest, preferably near cool, damp streambanks. It is circular in appearance, its bright green fronds accentu-  ated by black, shiny "wirelike" leafstalks. Look down for this beautiful fern, for it only grows a foot high, and rarely over two feet.

Lady Fern

This large and graceful fern thrives in the shady forests throughout the Northwest. Its favorite place is damp soils along native streambanks. While not quite as plentiful in Forest Park as the other fabulous four, it still is a fun fern to find, and easy to identify, too. It can grow tall—up to five feet—but generally is around two feet high. Its leaves have a styl-

ish quality—widest near the middle but evenly tapered toward the top and bottom. Interestingly, this lovely fern is not ever-green! Rather, it is decidu-ous. In fall, its verdant fronds turn brown, and the elegant lady fern will drop its leaves.

Licorice Fern

When one thinks of plants, we usually assume they grow in soil in the ground. This abundant fern, however, takes us by surprise! It prefers growing out of tree trunks. Look for it in the wet seasons of the year, flourishing thickly on heavy coverings of moss holding fast to bigleaf

maples in the park. In the dry season, it dies back, hence it is known as a "summer deciduous fern." The adaptable licorice fern holds other surprises as well. It also can grow out of what seems to be rocks. Where moss is adhering to eroded crevices on outcroppings of Columbia River Basalt in Forest Park, you will often find licorice ferns adorning the rocky exposures. A whiff of the root of a lico-rice fern can make you easily understand where the fern's name comes from; it has a decided smell of anise.

DOGWOOD AND WILD CHERRY TRAILS are joined at the start. After fifty yards, they split. At this spot there is a plaque dedicated to the memory of Larry Mauritz, who loved this trail. Its inscription captures the sentiments of what many feel about Forest Park: "Here rest your wings when they are weary. Here lodge as in a sanctuary."

Turn left and begin hiking on Dogwood Trail. Soon the trail turns sharply right and climbs up through the forest. For years, the viewpoint from this hill was known as "Inspiration Point" as it revealed panoramas of the Willamette River and the city of Portland. With the growth of trees through the decades, however, today the site is almost unidentifiable. Dogwood Trail dips down after the rise and gradually begins a descent that it maintains for its length.

After a half mile, Dogwood Trail intersects Wildwood Trail; continue downhill on lower Dogwood, which becomes steeper after this junction. At the intersection of Dogwood Trail with Leif Erikson Drive, turn left and begin hiking north. After another half mile, at Leif Erikson Milepost 1½, Alder Trail intersects the road, coming in from above and to the left. Turn left on Alder Trail and follow it as it ascends the canyon, next to a sparkling stream. Alder Trail is aptly named—red alder trees are abundant throughout and grow interspersed with bigleaf maples.

After about a mile, Alder Trail intersects Wildwood Trail. Turn left on Wildwood Trail and continue a quarter mile farther to an intersection with Keil Trail. Turn right on Keil Trail, named for William "Bill" Keil, the first Forest Park forester. Between 1952 and 1956, Keil was instrumental in developing a fire protection plan for the forest and helped create all the fire lanes that run throughout the park. Continue on Keil Trail for a quarter mile and merge right onto Dogwood Trail to return to the parking area, completing the loop.

HIKE 6
Firelane 7, Ridge Trail, Wildwood Trail, and Hardesty Trail Loop

DISTANCE: 2 miles
HIKING TIME: 1 hour
DIFFICULTY RATING: Easy
WATERSHED: Doane Creek Watershed; Springville Creek Watershed
TRAILHEAD: Springville Road

Foot traffic only on Ridge Trail, Hardesty Trail, and Wildwood Trail. Firelane 7 is also open to horses.

MILEAGE AND DIRECTIONS
0.0　Begin at Firelane 7 Trailhead at Springville Road.
0.4　Turn left at the junction with Ridge Trail. Hike Ridge Trail.
0.8　Intersection with Wildwood Trail. Turn left onto Wildwood Trail.
1.6　Hardesty Trail intersects Wildwood. Turn left onto Hardesty Trail.
1.9　Intersection with Firelane 7. Turn right.
2.0　End at Springville Road Parking Area.

This picturesque loop takes a hiker quickly into the heart of Forest Park. In particular, Ridge Trail offers cathedral trees and remarkable stillness that easily inspire a sense of awe and wonder. Many features of a natural Coast Range forest are evident—from blooming native shrubbery, chittering Douglas squirrels, to singing nuthatches and wrens—and can make one feel worlds away from busy, urban existence. Slow down, look around you, and find your sanctuary pause.

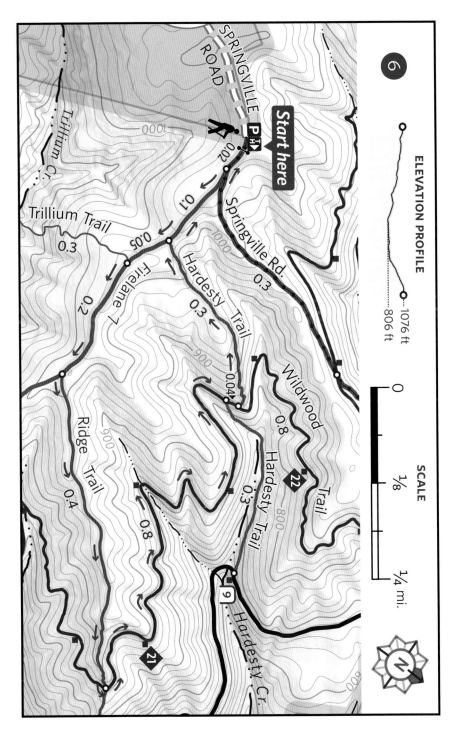

ELEVATION PROFILE

1076 ft

806 ft

SCALE

0   1/8   1/4 mi.

6

Start here

SPRINGVILLE ROAD

Trillium Cr.

Trillium Trail

0.3

0.2

Fireline

0.05

0.1

0.7

1000

Springville Rd.

0.3

Hardesty Trail

0.3

0.04

900

Ridge Trail

0.4

0.8

900

Wildwood Trail

0.8

Hardesty Trail

0.3

800

22

9

21

Hardesty Cr.

600

N

CAN YOU FIND?
A Plant for Valentine's Day

Every year around February 14, a native plant emerges and grows profusely in the Douglas-fir forest within in Forest Park: wild ginger. Especially in late winter or early spring, it's easy to identify. Its leathery leaves are shaped just like a heart. Look for it growing low to the ground.

It got its name because of its spicy fragrance, like that of ginger. The best time to find it is when other shrubs and plants in the forest have not yet leafed out, so it is highly visible—around Valentine's Day!

DID YOU KNOW?
Forest Park's Oregon Grape Is Not Our State Flower!

How is that? Because there's more than one species of Oregon grape! Two species are found in Oregon. Tall Oregon grape (*Berberis aquifolium*) is a larger variety that grows up to six feet high and occurs in more open forests and forest margins.

This variety is Oregon's state flower. The species that grows abundantly throughout Forest Park, however, and in the more moist forests of the Coast Range, is a low-growing shrub that thrives in deep shade: Cascade Oregon grape (*Berberis nervosa*). This plant is a hallmark of Douglas-fir forests. Be on the lookout for its yellow flowers in spring, and later, its purplish-blue berries that resemble little grapes.

DID YOU KNOW?

What Forest Park Tree Has One of the Largest Leaves of All Trees in North America?

Bigleaf maple—a tall, native tree that thrives in Forest Park. This tree has a leaf that resembles the shape of a hand and grows six to twelve inches across, or even larger. It has the largest leaf of all 128 species of maple trees on earth. Little wonder this grand tree is known as bigleaf maple!

CAN YOU FIND?

An Old Stump That Is Acting Like a Nurse for New Trees

Some species of trees, like western hemlocks, need a hand to get started in the forest. They have difficulty seeding themselves directly on the matted forest floor. This is where "nurse logs" come in! Fallen logs or remnants of Douglas-fir stumps, so common along Wildwood Trail, are teeming with life-giving nutrients. As they decompose, they make a perfect bed on which tree seedlings can begin to grow. Later these will become large, healthy trees!

TO BEGIN THE HIKE, pass the park gate. Two pathways soon split: Springville Road to the north and Firelane 7 to the south. Hike Firelane 7, passing several side trails, until reaching Ridge Trail on the left.

For the next half mile, Ridge Trail winds through impressive woods within the 695-acre Springville Creek Watershed. Canyons drop off on either side of the trail. This section is easy walking, with many native plants adorning the trail. This is one of Forest Park's most intact watersheds, from its headwaters near NW Skyline Boulevard to the point where it empties into a culvert, 1,000 feet below, where its stream water is piped under the highway and industrial area, and finally discharged into the Willamette River.

At the intersection of Ridge Trail and Wildwood Trail, turn left and continue on Wildwood Trail for three quarters of a mile. At the junction with Hardesty Trail, coming in from above, turn left, and travel on this short, rewarding path, which is slightly steep in parts. The trail was named for William Hardesty, a founding member of the Mazamas, a nonprofit mountaineering organization. For years, he dedicated his time following the ideals of the Mazama's constitution, written in 1896, working for the "preservation of the forests and other features of mountain scenery in their natural beauty." In 1944, the Portland chapter helped build this trail and dedicated it in Hardesty's honor.

Hardesty Trail emerges onto Firelane 7 after a quarter mile. Turn right onto the fire lane and return to the Springville Parking Area, completing the hike.

HIKE 7
Cannon Trail, Wildwood Trail, Waterline Trail, and Leif Erikson Loop

DISTANCE: 3 miles
HIKING TIME: 1.5 hours
DIFFICULTY RATING: Moderate
WATERSHED: Linnton Creek Watershed; Springville Creek Watershed
TRAILHEAD: Germantown Road/Leif Erikson Drive

Foot traffic only on Cannon Trail, Wildwood Trail, and Waterline Trail. Leif
Erikson Drive also allows bicycles and horses.

MILEAGE AND DIRECTIONS
0.0   Begin at Cannon Trail at Leif Erikson Parking Area. Hike Cannon.
0.3   Turn left on Wildwood.
0.9   Waterline Trail intersects Wildwood. Turn right on Upper Waterline
       Trail.
1.3   Waterline Trail ends at Watertower Meadow. Turn around and hike
       back to intersection with Wildwood Trail. Cross Wildwood and hike
       Lower Waterline Trail.
2.1   Lower Waterline Trail intersects with Leif Erikson Drive. Turn left on
       Leif Erikson.
3.1   Return to the Leif Erikson Parking Area.

This beautiful loop captures four things that are special about Forest Park:
It allows a close-up glimpse of a nearly intact, healthy watershed. It winds
through luxurious forest habitat indicative of the Western Hemlock Vegetation Zone, with graceful trees adorned by draping mosses. It gives a window
into the history of Forest Park and offers the chance to see the largest grassy
meadow, maintained by Portland Parks, within Forest Park. It is best hiked in
summer because the steeper pitches of Waterline Trail can become muddy
and slippery in winter.

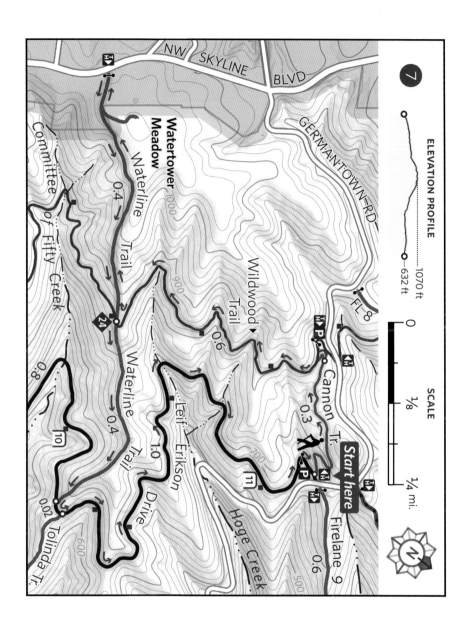

CAN YOU FIND?

What Pieces of Evidence Tell You You're on Waterline Trail?

Get ready for a scavenger hunt! Keep your eyes open on both sides of Waterline Trail—Upper and Lower. Can you find evidence of an old water pipe in the middle of the upper trail? What about the tall, space-age looking tower in the top meadow? That's Willalatin Watertank Tower, a giant, 200,000-gallon elevated water tank, built in 1968 by the Bureau of Water Works. Look further: Can you spy an orange fire hydrant somewhere in the meadow? And on the lower section of Waterline Trail, look for an old, square water valve alongside the path.

CAN YOU FIND?

A Prolific Plant That Appears to Completely Vanish in Forest Park in Winter!

Most of the year, native Pacific waterleaf can be found as a sprawling groundcover throughout much of Forest Park, especially in moist areas near creeks. It grows profusely from underground rhizomes and forms large carpets in the Douglas-fir forests of western Oregon, Washington, and British Columbia. Its leaves, two to twelve inches long and covered

with soft hairs that catch dew and rain drops, give the plant its name—*waterleaf.* Intriguingly, this luxurious vegetation dies completely back to its roots each year, effectively "disappearing" from our sight!

CAN YOU FIND?

Forest Park's Noisiest Mammal

Well-known for its noisy calls resembling high-pitched, repetitive chirps, Douglas squirrels frequent Forest Park. These active squirrels, native to West Coast Douglas-fir forests, are often seen running and leaping from tree limb to limb, almost as if they are playing. Easy to identify, they are grayish with reddish tones on their backs and pale orange on their chests. Forest Park provides a perfect home for them, as their preferred habitat is old-growth forests or mature second-growth forests, where they can forage their favorite food: seeds of coniferous trees.

DID YOU KNOW?

What Type of Plant Has Been Used for Centuries to Make Baskets, Ropes, Medicines, Treat Injuries, as well as Used for Insulation and Sealants in Traditional Log Houses?

Mosses! There are over 9,000 species of mosses in the world, and they can live on surfaces where vascular plants have difficulty surviving. Mosses grow on stones, bark, soil, rock walls, caves, tundra streams, and wetlands. Numerous species can be found in Forest Park, like this moss, which clings to the trunks and drapes over the branches of many trees you will pass on Wildwood and Waterline Trails.

TO BEGIN THE HIKE, head uphill on Cannon Trail. The trail is named for Garnet "Ding" Cannon, considered the "Father of Forest Park." A tireless advocate for the park's creation, in 1946, Cannon founded the Forest Park Committee of Fifty—a civic organization that began a plan of action to establish the park. After two years of intense work, the group met with success. A unique, wilderness park for Portland was created in 1948. For the next forty years, the remainder of his life, Cannon remained one of Forest Park's most committed supporters.

After a quarter mile, turn left onto Wildwood Trail. Hike Wildwood as it winds among towering Douglas-fir trees, until its intersection with Waterline Trail. Here, turn right onto Waterline Trail, and climb. This ridgeline trail is the dividing line between Springville Creek Watershed to the south and Linnton Creek Watershed to the north. From this vantage point, watershed health can be comprehended by understanding key features. The area has full forest cover, predominantly native, which helps to maintain biodiversity. The umbrella of vegetation helps to reduce the effects of erosion, works to mitigate flooding from seasonal rainfall, and provides the Willamette River, below, with cleaner inflow.

After a half mile, Waterline Trail ends at a grassy, open field—Watertower Meadow. This wide parkland area is a great place to pause and have a picnic. Continue the hike by returning down Waterline Trail. At its intersection with Wildwood Trail, cross Wildwood and descend Lower Waterline Trail, which, during wet seasons, can be very slippery in sections with several steep pitches. Lower Waterline Trail ends at Leif Erikson Drive. Turn left onto Leif Erikson. Saunter a mile along this country lane. The wide pathway returns to the parking area, completing the loop.

HIKE 8
HOYT ARBORETUM: Spruce Trail, Wildwood Trail, Barbara Walker
Crossing, and Redwood Trail Loop

DISTANCE: 2 miles
HIKING TIME: 1–1.5 hours
DIFFICULTY RATING: Easy
TRAILHEAD: Hoyt Arboretum Visitor Center

Foot traffic only.

MILEAGE AND DIRECTIONS
0.0   Begin at the Hoyt Arboretum Visitor Center. Cross Fairview Boulevard
      and turn right onto Fir Trail. At the first split, go left onto Spruce Trail.
0.4   Spruce Trail intersects with Wildwood Trail. Turn left onto
      Wildwood Trail and hike to Barbara Walker Crossing.
0.9   If not hiking to Pittock Mansion, which is 0.6 miles farther, turn
      around here. Return on Wildwood Trail until its intersection with
      Redwood Trail, which is directly under the Redwood Deck. Turn
      right on Redwood Trail for 0.5 miles. Redwood crosses Fischer Lane.
      Continue on Redwood Trail.
1.7   Redwood Trail intersects with Fir Trail. Turn left on Fir Trail to reach
      the Stevens Pavilion. Cross Fairview Boulevard to return to the visitor
      center.

Hoyt Arboretum is a living museum featuring trees and plants collected from
all parts of the globe. It is located on a ridgetop above Washington Park on
traditional land of the Atfalati, Chinook, and Cowlitz people. Established
in 1928, it offers twelve miles of scenic, peaceful hiking trails traversing 189
acres. Showcasing more than 2,300 tree species and cultivars from six continents, including sixty-seven that are rare and endangered, Hoyt Arboretum
is an important conservator of the earth's biodiversity, as well as a center for
botanical education. Over 6,000 of its trees and shrubs are labeled, with common and scientific names and native habitats. As our planet continues to
lose native species to extinction, Hoyt Arboretum plays an invaluable role in
furthering scientific understanding, safeguarding valuable genetic material,
and preserving diversity on a global level.

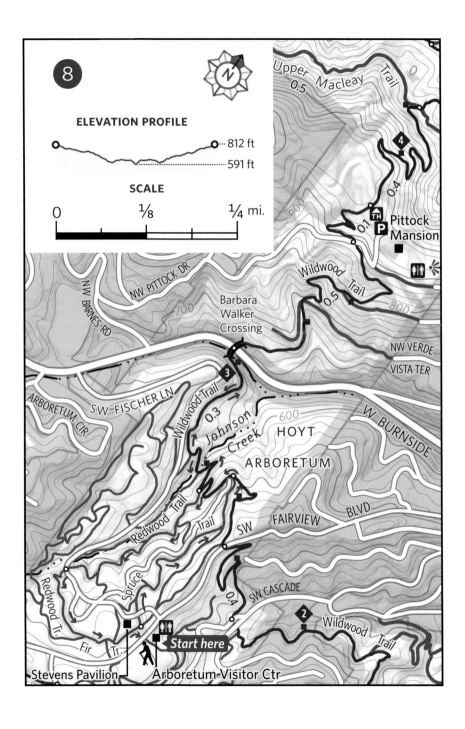

ELEVATION PROFILE

812 ft
591 ft

SCALE

0   1/8   1/4 mi.

Upper Macleay Trail
0.5

4

0.4

0.1 TH P Pittock Mansion

Wildwood Trail
0.5

NW PITTOCK DR

NW BARNES RD

700

Barbara Walker Crossing

800

NW VERDE VISTA TER

3

Wildwood Trail
0.3

ARBORETUM CIR.

S.W. FISCHER LN.

Johnson Creek

600

HOYT ARBORETUM

W. BURNSIDE

Redwood Trail

Trail

SW FAIRVIEW BLVD

SW

0.4

SW CASCADE

2

Wildwood Trail

Spruce

Redwood Tr.

Fir Tr.

Stevens Pavilion

Start here

Arboretum Visitor Ctr

DID YOU KNOW?

What Recent Structure Has Allowed Safe Passage Across a Dangerous Highway?

The Barbara Walker Crossing! This artistic, vibrant, and imaginative pedestrian bridge overarches busy West Burnside Street and was built to connect Wildwood Trail as it exits Hoyt Arboretum and enters Forest Park. For decades, hikers had to dash across Burnside Street, often taking their lives in hand, to make it to the other side. Designed by architect Ed Carpenter and completed in 2019, this award-wining span now allows safe passage. It is named in honor of Barbara Walker, a longtime advocate for Portland parks and natural areas, who helped save Marquam Park from development and resurrected the Olmsted Brothers' vision of a preserved nature loop around Portland, the "40-Mile Loop," which today has grown to over 140 miles!

"Nothing is going to be more valuable than having a connection with nature in our cities, and an attachment to the earth. If we can keep nature in our cities, we can create the most wonderful communities ever."—Barbara Walker

DID YOU KNOW?

What Tree in Hoyt Arboretum is Known as a Living Fossil?

The dawn redwood (*Metasequoia glyptostroboides*)! During the Miocene Period (5 to 25 million years ago) it was widespread across much of the Northern Hemisphere but then vanished. For years it was only known from the fossil record. Then, in the 1940s, a small grove was identified near a rural village in central China. Seeds were sent to Arnold Arboretum at Harvard University, which distributed them to several botanic gardens. Hoyt Arboretum received a batch of fifty seeds in 1950. Years later,

one of these trees became the first dawn redwood to produce reproductive cones in the Western Hemisphere for millions of years!

CAN YOU FIND?

Salal

A common shrub of the Douglas-fir forest is salal. It is one of three that are indicative of this ecosystem, along with Oregon grape and sword fern. Look for a dense ground cover with thick, oval, leathery leaves and growing about one to three feet tall. Salal has bell-shaped flowers that, when they turn into fruit, resemble blueberries. It is an important plant to Indigenous peoples, who use the berries to make a blue dye.

AT EVERY SEASON OF THE YEAR, Hoyt Arboretum offers something new to appreciate among its three nationally recognized collections. In spring, flowering trees in the Magnolia Collection, together with numerous varieties of cherry and dogwood trees, set the hillsides abloom. In summer, the Conifer Collection, located north of Fairview Boulevard, has hundreds of pines, firs, cedars, spruces, sequoias, and hemlocks, all providing welcome shade on a warm day. In fall, exquisite crimson, orange, and yellow leaves highlight the Maple Collection, where maples, oaks, beeches, and ashes create some of the most spectacular scenery in all of Portland. In winter, over 140 varieties of holly light up the trails with splashes of bright red berries.

While a myriad of routes can be chosen to explore Hoyt Arboretum, for an easy, two-mile loop that captures its beauty and diversity begin at the visitor center. Cross Fairview Boulevard and head towards the Stevens Pavilion, a large, covered picnic shelter, where Fir Trail begins. Head north on this trail until its intersection with Spruce Trail. Turn left onto Spruce Trail, which travels through the Arboretum's Conifer Collection, featuring one of the largest assemblages of coniferous trees in the world, with over 260 species collected from six continents.

Spruce Trail ends at a junction with Wildwood Trail near the end of Bray Lane. Turn left onto Wildwood Trail and proceed to the Redwood Deck and Overlook, an oasis with a large platform situated among a magnificent grove of tall, straight-trunked redwoods. Three distinct redwood species can be observed: Giant Sequoia—the largest of all trees in bulk and most massive living things by volume; Coast Redwood—the tallest living trees; and the deciduous Dawn Redwood. The first redwoods in the Arboretum were planted in 1931.

Continue on Wildwood Trail as it curves down the ravine to the canyon bottom, where it crosses over a bridge above Johnson Creek. Beyond this point, the vegetation is now maintained as a natural area and highlights plants native to the Douglas-fir region of western Oregon. A half-mile farther, Wildwood Trail approaches the Barbara Walker Crossing—the new pedestrian bridge and one-of-a-kind architectural display that spans West Burnside Street, allowing safe passage across the busy highway.

If desiring a longer walk, continue uphill on Wildwood Trail for 0.6 miles, until reaching the Pittock Mansion. (See Hike 2.) For the purposes of this hike, however, turn around here. Return on Wildwood, retracing steps and crossing over the bridge once more. After the bridge crossing, Wildwood

Trail intersects Creek Trail, which comes in on the right. Bear sharply left to continue on Wildwood until its intersection with Redwood Trail, located just beneath the Redwood Deck. Turn right onto Redwood Trail. Follow the easy-walking, lower trail as it winds through the Arboretum next to Johnson Creek. In 0.5 miles, Redwood Trail crosses SW Fischer Lane; it continues on the other side of the lane. Stay on Redwood Trail until it ends at Fir Trail. Turn left onto Fir, which leads to the Stevens Pavilion. From here, cross Fairview once again and return to the visitor center, completing the loop.

HIKE 9
BPA Road to Firelane 13 Overlook

DISTANCE: 2.4 miles
HIKING TIME: 1.5 hours
DIFFICULTY RATING: Easy
WATERSHED: Newton Creek Watershed; Miller Creek Watershed
TRAILHEAD: BPA Road/Skyline Boulevard

Foot traffic only on Firelane 13. BPA Road also allows bicycles and horses.

MILEAGE AND DIRECTIONS
0.0   Begin at BPA Road Trailhead, just off Skyline Boulevard. Hike BPA Road.
0.5   Cross Wildwood Trail. Continue on BPA.
0.8   Intersect Firelane 12. Continue on BPA.
1.2   At junction with Firelane 13, turn left. Hike to overlook. For return trip, retrace steps.
2.4   End at BPA Road Trailhead.

For anyone desiring an outing with commanding views of mountains and rivers on trails less traveled, and an especially great one to do with kids, this is a fun one to try. The path follows under powerlines for much of its length and provides the chance to see wildlife often hidden among the trees. Be watchful for red-tailed hawks soaring above, and turkey vultures congregating in the lower reaches. Tracks of black-tailed deer and coyotes are frequently observable in muddy spots along the ridgetops. Firelane 13 climbs to a sweeping overlook. Currently, the site is being monitored for its native butterflies and bees and is part of the exciting Forest Park Pollinator Powerline Project, headed by the Xerces Society.

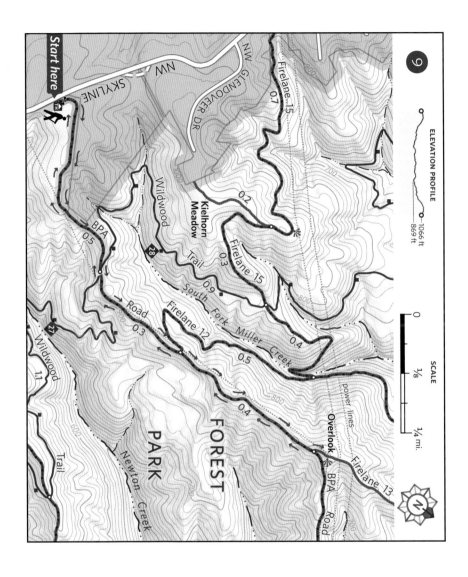

DID YOU KNOW?

How Many Bites of Food That You Eat Exist because of the Work of Pollinators?

One out of every three bites! The food you eat depends on pollinators—bees, butterflies, flies, moths, and birds—doing their jobs to collect and move pollen through the landscape. Pollinators transport pollen, the plant's male sex cells, to female parts of plants. It's what allows plants to reproduce and make fruits and seeds.

CAN YOU FIND?

What's That Track?

Nature tracking can be fun! And the place to look is in muddy spots along the ridgetops and fire lanes in Forest Park. One track easy to identify is that of black-tailed deer. These native deer frequent the park and occur in small family groups or small groups of bucks. Their tracks, though, are generally more visible than the animals themselves, and are a give-away that they were here. Look for the imprint of their two-hoofed toes that together form what appears to be the shape of a heart.

CAN YOU FIND?

An Animal in Forest Park That Can See a Mouse from 100 Feet Up in the Air and Then Dive Up to 120 Miles Per Hour to Catch It!

Keep your eyes peeled for a common, widely distributed bird in Forest Park: a red-tailed hawk! This raptor can often be seen soaring high above transmission powerlines and fire lanes. Red-tailed hawks have terrific "binocular" vision, which means both of their eyes work together to see  prey from far away and also allows them to focus quickly when they dive. Like other raptors, they have a third eyelid, called a "nictitating membrane." This "lid" moves from side to side and keeps the eye clean and moist, aiding their superb vision.

DID YOU KNOW?

What Percentage of Flowering Plants Depend on Pollinators?

 Close to 90 percent of flowering plant species depend on animal pollination! Also, almost 75 percent of leading global crops require pollination from bees, the leading pollinators, and other animal pollinators.

BPA ROAD BEGINS as a pretty, grassy lane that passes through a tree-lined corridor under a canopy of red alder trees. At first, it undulates gently, and then opens up as it approaches the powerlines. Cleared of trees to allow access for transmission poles, the road reveals fine views of Mt. Rainier and Mt. St. Helens and the confluence of the Willamette and Columbia Rivers. After approximately a half mile, BPA Road crosses Wildwood Trail. Stay on BPA Road, which continues down the ridgeline. This road is the separation point between two significant watersheds in Forest Park. On the left (north) of BPA Road is Miller Creek Watershed; on the right (south) is Newton Creek Watershed. Deep within these forested ravines remnant stands of old-growth trees can still be found.

A quarter mile past the intersection of Wildwood Trail, Firelane 12 intersects BPA Road on the left. Wildflowers abound along the path. Remain on BPA Road until it forks at a major junction underneath several powerlines. Here, veer left on Firelane 13 and climb uphill.

At the crest of the hilltop, Firelane 13 affords one of the most far-reaching overlooks in Forest Park. Even though the view is compromised by a network of powerlines, it's worth taking the time to pause and look around. Rural Sauvies Island and Mt. St. Helens, Mt. Rainier, and Mt. Adams are observable and offset by the curving blue courses of the Willamette and Columbia Rivers and Multnomah Channel. This is a sanctioned Wildlife Habitat Area in Forest Park, which is being regenerated with native flowering plants for the benefit of butterflies, bees, birds, and other pollinators. METRO, the Xerces Society, Portland Parks and Recreation, and the Bonneville Power Association are all working together to help increase populations of essential pollinators, which are experiencing serious declines around the globe.

For the return trip, retrace your steps to BPA Road and to the trailhead.

HIKE 10
Newton Road, Wildwood Trail to Germantown Road

DISTANCE: 3 miles
HIKING TIME: 1.5 hours
DIFFICULTY RATING: Easy
WATERSHED: Linnton Creek Watershed
TRAILHEAD: Newton Road/Skyline Boulevard

Foot traffic only on Wildwood Trail. Newton Road also allows bicycles and horses.

MILEAGE AND DIRECTIONS
0.0   Begin at Newton Road Trailhead. Hike to intersection with Wildwood Trail.
0.6   Turn right onto Wildwood Trail.
2.2   Arrive at Germantown Road. Turn around.
2.9   Intersection with Firelane 10. Turn left on Firelane 10.
3.1   Arrive at Newton Road Trailhead.

This easy hike is a great introduction to the superb North Unit of Forest Park. The portion of Wildwood Trail between Newton and Germantown Roads captures the peace, solitude, and tranquility that symbolize Forest Park. In addition, it is more easily accessible than some sections of Wildwood Trail. This hike is wonderful to do with children; it is not difficult and gives a good introduction to the wonders of a western Oregon coniferous forest. Even more impressive for a city of Portland's size, the vegetation and wildlife are overwhelmingly native in these woods and provide an exceptional educational experience without having to drive to distant locations to find natural habitat. As a bonus, the hike crosses several important streams flowing freely during the winter and after rainstorms. Together, they act to augment the high functioning of the 855-acre Linnton Creek Watershed.

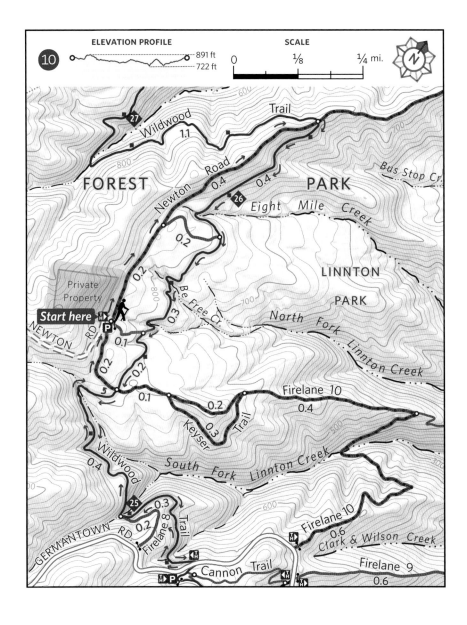

ELEVATION PROFILE

10
891 ft
722 ft

SCALE

0   1/8   1/4 mi.

27
Wildwood
1.1

FOREST

Newton
Road
0.4   0.4

800

PARK

Bus Stop Cr.

26
Eight   Mile   Creek

0.2

LINNTON

PARK

Private
Property

Start here

NEWTON RD

800
Be Free Cr.
0.3

700

North   Fork   Linnton Creek

0.2

0.1

0.2

0.2

0.1

Firelane 10
0.4

0.2
Keyser   0.3   Trail

South   Fork   Linnton Creek

300

Wildwood
0.4

600

25
0.3
0.2
Firelane 8   Trail

GERMANTOWN RD

Cannon   Trail

Firelane 10
0.6
Clark & Wilson   Creek

Firelane 9
0.6

DID YOU KNOW?
What Is a "Mother Tree"?

Scientists have discovered that trees can communicate with each other—transmitting their needs and sending each other nutrients—via a remarkable network of latticed fungi buried in the soil! Below-ground fungi send threads, called mycelium, throughout the soil. These connect one tree root system to another. Acting like a pipeline, they can send carbon, water, and nutrients back and forth. In the forest, the biggest, oldest trees have the most connections to other trees because they have more roots. Termed "Mother Trees," they have been shown to use the network to nurture their own seedlings that they can recognize!

CAN YOU FIND?
The Most Common Amphibian in Forest Park

All the amphibians in Forest Park are native, but few species occur due to a lack of ponds. Several, however, are well-distributed and abundant near Forest Park streams and where there is large woody debris and where they can hide under logs. The most likely species to find is the Ensatina salamander. Three to five inches long, they can be identi-

fied by having five toes on their back feet. Don't pick them up, though. They are easily distressed, and their thin skin is very sensitive to chemicals from warm hands.

CAN YOU FIND?
A Plant with Leaves Looking Like They're Riding Piggyback!

Native to moist forests of Western Oregon and Washington, the piggyback plant is a fun plant to search for *and* is an important part of our natural Douglas-fir forests! In the spring, look close to the ground. Piggyback plant grows only 1 to 1.5 feet tall, and in mats. Its bright green leaf is triangular. What makes it special, though, is that it produces a second set of little leaves growing on top of the first. It looks almost like a baby being carried, hence its other popular name, *youth–on–age*!

CAN YOU FIND?
Who Has Walked This Path Before?

Trail plant holds some answers. The low-growing plant's leaf is a green triangle above but is white underneath. When someone passes through a patch and knocks the plant, the leaf often flips over. It shows its underside, which looks like a white marker. Historically, trackers could figure out where a person had passed through an area by following these markers, thereby explaining the plants other common name, *pathfinder*.

BEGIN THE HIKE by walking around the northern gate on the continuation of Newton Road. (The gate to the south leads to Firelane 10.) Initially, the grade of Newton Road is gentle, but soon climbs uphill sharply. After this rise, however, the trail levels out again for easy walking. Along this section, notice the deep coniferous forest that stretches to the north. This is the border of the beautiful Newton Creek Watershed. Here, in isolated pockets, majestic old-growth trees, giant downed logs, and large snags can be found. All of these features are remnants of the old-growth forest that historically covered much of Forest Park.

After slightly more than a half mile, Newton Road intersects with Wildwood Trail. Turn right on Wildwood Trail. Almost immediately the natural habitat surrounds you with lots to observe. Nearly all of the trees, shrubs, and flowers are native to and indicative of the Western Hemlock Vegetation Zone, making Forest Park an excellent place to learn about them.

Five species of ferns—sword, lady, licorice, maidenhair, and bracken—grow vigorously in spots. Oregon grape, red huckleberry, osoberry, and other native shrubs grow robustly. Native plants, such as Solomon's plume, fringe-cup, Hooker's fairy bells, and fairy lanterns, can be seen under young western red cedars, western hemlock trees, and tall bigleaf maples. At Milepost 26¼, a few spectacular old-growth Douglas-firs can be observed growing next to the trail.

Near Milepost 26, the trail crosses a major stream, Eight Mile Creek, named for a Pittmon Map description defining this location as being eight miles from the center of downtown Portland in 1946—the same time Forest Park was created. A quarter mile farther is another stream crossing—Be Free Creek. It can be recognized by a trailside rock monument with the inscription, "Be Free Where You Are." This tribute is in the memory of Gaelle Snell, who loved Forest Park.

Throughout this section of Wildwood Trail numerous bird species are prevalent at different times of the year and are native to this ecosystem. A number of these birds are Special Status Species and in decline; they depend on the important habitat that Forest Park offers. Look for golden-crowned kinglets, song sparrows, brown creepers, chestnut-backed chickadees, varied thrushes, red-breasted nuthatches, and winter wrens. In summer, Pacific-slope flycatchers, Swainson's thrushes, black-throated gray warblers, and western tanagers can be heard in the trees. Also listen for the characteristic chatter of two common native mammals that range throughout Forest Park: Douglas squirrels and Townsend's chipmunks.

Just before Milepost 25¼, a park bench honoring Bruno Kolkowsky is situated next to the trail. A longtime volunteer and steward of the park, Kolkowsky gave hundreds of hours of his time to build and maintain its trails. This section of Wildwood was in a large measure built by volunteers, and predominantly by Kolkowsky, who worked closely with Fred Nilsen, Forest Park arboriculturist, and another dedicated volunteer, Bill Sauerwein. This bench tells of Kolkowsky's enduring commitment to the park with the inscription "This Trail Is His Legacy."

Wildwood Trail crosses Linnton Creek at Milepost 25. Soon the trail begins to climb upward to Germantown Road. On this rising hill, look down into Linnton Creek Canyon for a sanctuary pause. A half mile from the creek crossing, Wildwood reaches Germantown Road. Here, turn around, head north, and retrace your steps once again on Wildwood Trail. At the intersection of Wildwood with Firelane 10, turn left on Firelane 10. This spur trail soon leads back to the trailhead at Newton Road Parking Area, completing the hike.

Great Hikes for Wildflowers

HIKE 11
Firelane 7, Trillium Trail, Wildwood Trail, and Ridge Trail Loop

DISTANCE: 3.5 miles
HIKING TIME: 2 hours
DIFFICULTY RATING: Moderate
WATERSHED: Doane Creek Watershed; Springville Creek Watershed
TRAILHEAD: Springville Road

Foot traffic only on Trillium Trail, Wildwood Trail, and Ridge Trail.
Firelane 7 is also open for horses, but no bicycles are permitted.

MILEAGE AND DIRECTIONS
0.0   Begin at Firelane 7. Hike 0.2 miles until its intersection with Trillium
      Trail. Turn right onto Trillium Trail.
0.5   Trillium Trail intersects Wildwood Trail. Turn left onto Wildwood
      Trail.
2.8   Wildwood Trail intersects with Ridge Trail. Turn left onto Ridge Trail.
3.2   Ridge Trail ends at Firelane 7. Turn right on Firelane 7.
3.5   End at Springville Road Parking Area.

This beautiful hike is aptly named: in spring these trails abound with showy trilliums—the graceful, native flower that, under natural conditions, grows luxuriantly throughout the forest, in places creating carpets of white. In cool, wet sections of trail, there are scores of other native plants to enjoy, many emerging at different times of year. Oregon oxalis, Pacific waterleaf, clasping twisted stalk, Hooker's fairy bells, fairy lanterns, Solomon's plume, and fringecup all grow abundantly. As an added bonus, Wildwood Trail offers impressive views into deep canyons of Douglas-fir, hemlock, and cedar trees in the Doane Creek Watershed, with some stands of old trees making one feel they are entering primeval woods. Sparkling Trillium Creek follows along for part of the way, lending the soothing sound of water along the path.

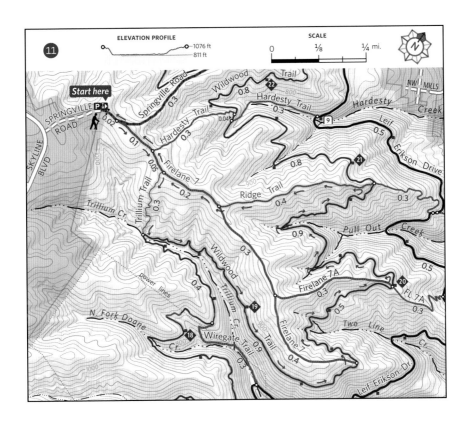

CAN YOU FIND?

The Showstopper of Early Spring!

To locate the one flower that heralds springtime more than any other, think "three-three-three." Forest Park's beautiful, native western trillium has them all: three leaves, three petals, three sepals (the green outer parts of a flower that enclose a developing bud). Its bounty of white petals can light up

the floor of the forest. Trilliums grow in large patches where they can seem to turn the ground nearly white! As the flower ages, the petals also change color, from snowy white to pink, and at last, to purple.

CAN YOU FIND?

A Plant with a Leaf Resembling the Foot of a Duck!

(Hint: Its Small White Flowers also Look Like Umbrellas)

Native duck's foot, sometimes called inside-out flower, grows prolifically in Forest Park. It is a key species in shady Douglas-fir forests. Plus, it's a fun one to identify because its light green leaves are shaped like the splayed foot of a duck. Another easy way to recognize it is to look closely at its dainty, small, white flowers. When blooming, they resemble tiny white umbrellas or even a flower that appears to be inside out!

CAN YOU FIND?
Forest Park's Tallest Lily

Perhaps Forest Park's most flashy and flamboyant native plant is the "tiger" or Columbian lily. This wildflower is tall—growing three to five feet and more—and blooms along sunnier, wider pathways in Forest Park, such as the fire lanes. It is hard to miss in June, for its beautiful flower is unmistakable: bright orange with well-defined dark brown spots. The question an alert observer might ask: Since tigers are orange with black stripes, would this Forest Park flower be better named the jaguar lily?

DID YOU KNOW?
Trees Have Healing Powers!

Research shows that when we walk among woods and trees, we are receiving hosts of health benefits. Trees release antimicrobial essential oils that protect the trees themselves but also boost our own immune system. Strolling mindfully in the forest has been shown to reduce our blood pressure, heart rate, stress, anxiety, and feelings of confusion, as well as fight cancer. First introduced in Japan, *shinrin yoku*, or "forest bathing," is a medical therapy that is now being used worldwide to help improve health and wellbeing, increase creativity, and fight depression. Basically, we all feel better when we are in nature!

BEGIN THE HIKE by walking around a locked park gate and veer to the right onto Firelane 7. Firelane 7 follows the dividing ridgeline between two watersheds: Doane Creek (1,037 acres) to the south and Springville Creek (695 acres) to the north. After passing Hardesty Trail, coming in on the left, Trillium Trail soon intersects on the right. While a lovely, short trail, it is less developed and is steep in sections with some exposed roots. For an easier route, continue on Firelane 7 until its end at Wildwood, approximately a mile downhill. For this loop, though, turn right onto Trillium Trail and walk on switchbacks for a quarter mile until you intersect with Wildwood Trail.

Turn left on Wildwood Trail, and hike along a beautiful section next to Trillium Creek. After a mile, the trail winds through an exceptionally scenic grove of fir, cedar, and hemlock—a good place for a sanctuary pause.

The stretch of Wildwood Trail between Mileposts 20 and 20¾ contours in and out of Pull Out Creek Canyon. It crosses two waterways: South Fork Pull Out Creek, just past 20¼, and North Fork Pull Out Creek at 20.5. Along this section, the trail's V-shape provides a good visual explanation why there is a seeming length disparity between the seven-mile-long park, as the crow flies, and Wildwood Trail, which is much longer, at thirty miles in length. This difference can be explained because the park is steeply incised by eleven major watersheds. Wildwood Trail traverses in and out of Forest Park's canyons, crossing stream after stream, as it winds from one end of the park to the other. Moreover, for fun geographical reference, Pull Out Creek is the same creek than can be observed far below at the parking area on the south ramp of the St. Johns Bridge.

Just before Milepost 21, Ridge Trail intersects Wildwood Trail on the left coming in from above. Turn left on Ridge Trail and ascend the path. The half-mile trail is a picturesque combination of towering conifers mixed with graceful archways made of draping branches of native vine maple covered with mosses.

Continue on Ridge Trail for a half mile until its intersection with Firelane 7. Turn right onto the fire lane, which returns to the parking area, completing the loop.

HIKE 12
Firelane 1, Wildwood Trail, Chestnut Trail, and Nature Trail Loop

DISTANCE: 3.5 miles
HIKING TIME: 1.5 hours
DIFFICULTY RATING: Moderate
WATERSHED: Saltzman Creek Watershed
TRAILHEAD: Upper Firelane 1

Foot traffic only on Wildwood Trail, Chestnut Trail, and Nature Trail. Firelane 1 also allows bicycles and horses.

MILEAGE AND DIRECTIONS
0.0   Begin at the Firelane 1 Trailhead at the gated parking area off Forest Lane.
0.4   Wildwood Trail intersects Firelane 1. Turn left on Wildwood Trail.
1.0   Intersect spur to Nature Trail. Stay on Wildwood Trail.
1.3   Turn right onto Chestnut Trail.
1.8   Turn right on Leif Erikson Drive.
1.9   Turn right on Nature Trail.
2.9   Intersection with Firelane 1. Turn right.
3.0   Turn left on Wildwood Trail.
3.5   Turn right on Morak Trail.
3.6   Turn left on Firelane 1.
3.7   End at Firelane 1 Parking Area.

This peaceful medley of well-maintained trails offers beauty, solitude, and natural features of educational value and a relatively gentle terrain. Displays of numerous flowering shrubs, including elderberry, osoberry, red flowering currant, and salmonberry line the trails, as well as bountiful licorice, sword, lady, and maidenhair ferns. Several uncommon coniferous trees can be seen, including Pacific yew. As an added bonus, South and North Fork Rocking Chair Creeks accompany these trails and in early spring, are decorated with sprightly yellow wood violets, all within the highly scenic Saltzman Creek Watershed.

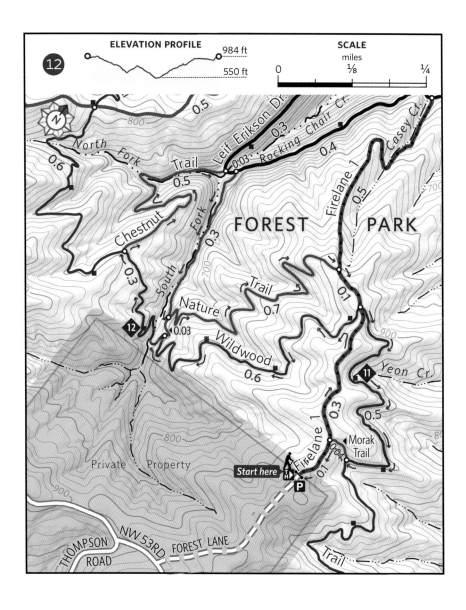

CAN YOU FIND?

The Shrub Whose Flowers Announce Spring

Osoberry is hard to miss in early February when almost all other plants have not even leafed out in Forest Park. It is the Northwest's earliest blooming native shrub. Osoberry's small, five-petaled white flowers hang down in clusters, and often appear before the plant's leaves have unfurled. It grows  from four to twelve feet tall and can be found along many of the trails in Forest Park. Later in the season, it displays fruit resembling small plums. (Beware, they're bitter!) Indigenous people routinely used the osoberry's fruit, twigs, and bark for food, teas, and medicines.

CAN YOU FIND?

When Is a Raspberry not a Raspberry?

When it's a thimbleberry! In summer, when berries are ripening in the forest, this common native shrub bears a strong resemblance to its cultivated cousin, the red raspberries we all enjoy. But while raspberries have  canes that are thorny, the branches of the thimbleberry are just fuzzy. Even more characteristic, the leaf of the wild thimbleberry, shaped like a maple leaf, is extremely soft. And the fruit? When ripe, it is very red, shaped like a little cap, edible, and tasty!

CAN YOU FIND?
The Forest Shrub That's Named after a Fish

Native to moist forests of the Northwest and found predominantly along streams, salmonberry is a vigorous shrub, growing up to ten feet tall, that thrives in natural Douglas-fir forests. Its bark is covered with fine prickles, and in spring, purplish-pink flowers burst to life and give color to the forest. Native birds and mammals feast on its orange berries—the color of salmon—that give the plant its common name. Indigenous people often ate the berries with salmon roe.

CAN YOU FIND?
Forest Park's American Chestnut Tree: One of the Last

At the end of Chestnut Trail stands an American chestnut tree. It may not look too grand right now, but a little over a century ago, American chestnuts were considered the nation's premier timber tree and numbered over 3 billion in North America! In 1904, however, a devastating

blight was accidentally introduced and wiped out American chestnuts from most of their range. This tree found in Forest Park, planted by forester Fred Cleator seventy-five years ago, is a surviving specimen in a region still free from the chestnut blight.

TO BEGIN THE LOOP, hike down Firelane 1 to reach the Wildwood trailhead. At this junction, turn left (north) onto Wildwood Trail. The trail gently descends into a forested canyon. In slightly over a half mile, a side trail, coming in from the right, joins Wildwood. This is a tie trail leading to Nature Trail. For a shorter hike, leave Wildwood at this point and proceed right on the tie trail, then right again on Nature Trail, which loops back one mile to the parking area. For the main loop, however, continue on Wildwood Trail. At the bottom of the ravine, cross South Fork Rocking Chair Creek, where young hemlock trees are thriving—growing out of the remnants of old Douglas-fir stumps. Numerous fallen logs of older Douglas-fir trees can be observed in Forest Park. Many of these old stumps act as "nurses" for new trees. Western hemlock trees, in particular, have difficulty seeding themselves directly on the matted forest floor. The bare top of a fallen log or tree stump in its early stages of decay, however, teeming with nutrients and decomposing humus made from the decay of twigs and needles falling from above, create a perfect bed on which tree seedlings can begin to grow.

After passing over the creek, continue uphill on Wildwood Trail. Beyond Milepost 12, Chestnut Trail joins Wildwood from the right. Turn right onto Chestnut Trail and descend a narrowing canyon along several switchbacks. Part way down the ravine, the path parallels North Fork Rocking Chair Creek, an exceptionally pretty stream. Pronounced exposures of Columbia River Basalt are visible along the walls of the stream. This bedrock was originally fluid lava spewed 16 million years ago from fissures in southeastern Washington and northeastern Oregon. It covers tens of thousands of square miles and underlies much of the Tualatin Mountain Range.

In a half mile, Chestnut Trail ends at Leif Erikson Drive. A rare, large American chestnut tree, planted by conservationist and forester Fred Cleator in the early 1950s, grows at this junction and is the namesake of Chestnut Trail. Turn right and walk on Leif Erikson a few hundred feet then turn right again onto Nature Trail.

Proceed uphill on Nature Trail, which follows South Fork Rocking Chair Creek and passes over several footbridges. There are several myths of how Rocking Chair Creek got its name. The truth behind the name is slightly more prosaic than romantic, however: it arose from a park employee's discovery, long ago, of a lone rocking chair lodged in the creek near Leif Erikson Drive.

At different seasons of the year, look for key plants all along Nature Trail—Pacific waterleaf, clasping twisted stalk, piggyback plant, foam flower, fringecups, and fairy lanterns—all native to moist Douglas-fir forests.

Nature Trail ends after one mile at a grassy meadow at Firelane 1. Veer right and ascend Firelane 1, climbing up the hill until intersecting once again with Wildwood Trail. Turn left (south) on Wildwood Trail. Almost immediately, the deep woods become more open and are dominated by alder trees interspersed with young conifers. At Milepost 11, Wildwood crosses Yeon Creek, an intermittent stream. A quarter mile farther, Wildwood Trail is intersected by Morak Trail. Turn right onto Morak Trail, named for volunteer Robert Morak, who for years painted all the wooden signs that helped guide visitors traveling through the forest. This short, winding path connects to Upper Firelane 1. At the intersection with Firelane 1, turn left to return to the parking area, completing the loop.

Great Hikes for Birdwatching

HIKE 13
Portland Audubon's Pittock Bird Sanctuary: Jay Trail Loop

DISTANCE: 1 mile
HIKING TIME: 1 hour
DIFFICULTY RATING: Easy
WATERSHED: Balch Creek Watershed
TRAILHEAD: Portland Audubon Interpretive Center

Foot traffic only.

MILEAGE AND DIRECTIONS
0.0   Begin at Portland Audubon Interpretive Center. Hike Jay Trail. Cross Balch Creek. Pass Wren Trail. Stay on Jay Trail.
0.6   Turn left on Woodpecker Trail.
0.8   Turn left and reconnect with Jay Trail.
1.0   Return on Jay Trail to Audubon Interpretive Center.

The Pittock Bird Sanctuary at Portland Audubon is a great way to become surrounded by birds and wildlife in a refuge just minutes from downtown Portland. It is one of three wildlife sanctuaries—including Uhtoff Sanctuary and Collins Sanctuary—located in Portland Audubon's 172 acres, nestled next to Forest Park. Over eighty species of birds use the area for breeding or for migration stopovers. Located in the heart of the Balch Creek Watershed, wildlife can be observed along Balch Creek, which flows for a mile through the sanctuary. Portland Audubon features over four miles of trails to explore and connects to eighty miles of Forest Park trails. Jay Trail, in the Pittock Sanctuary, is an easy introduction to the wonders of a natural temperate rainforest, including the opportunity to see a beautiful stand of old-growth Douglas-firs—remnants of the giants that once stood throughout much of western Oregon, Washington, and British Columbia.

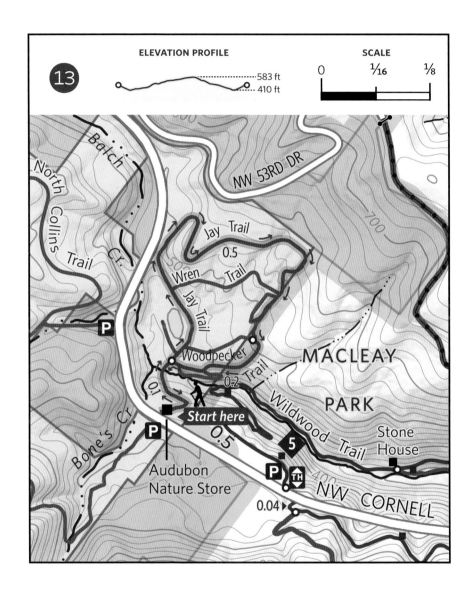

ELEVATION PROFILE

13

583 ft
410 ft

SCALE

0   1/16   1/8

NW 53RD DR

North Collins Trail

Balch

Cr.

Jay Trail

0.5

Wren   Trail

Jay Trail

P

Woodpecker

0.1

Bone's Cr.

Trail

0.2

Start here

0.5

P

Audubon
Nature Store

Wildwood   Trail

MACLEAY

PARK

Stone
House

5

P

TH

0.04 ▸

NW CORNELL

700

DID YOU KNOW?

What Animal Breathes Through Its Skin and Can Growl?

Pacific giant salamanders! This aquatic salamander species, when grown, breathes through its skin! It lives throughout Balch Creek and goes into the water to breed, then hides its eggs in logs, under rocks, or in streambeds. Mature Pacific giant salamanders reside in the dirt and leaf litter in moist forests. They are the Northwest's heaviest native salamander, can grow to be ten to thirteen inches long, and, if harassed, can reportedly growl at the invader!

DID YOU KNOW?

Who Eats the Bugs and Why Is That So Important?

Like this downy woodpecker who lives throughout Forest Park, woodpeckers play a critical role in the health of our forests. Five species of woodpeckers live in Forest Park. Because they are insectivorous, these native birds exert constant and critical pressure on insect populations, which helps prevent insects from reaching epidemic levels. Woodpeckers will consume between 24 to 98 percent of a beetle population at moderate to high beetle densities!

DID YOU KNOW?

What Bird Has Helped Make Better Crash Helmets for Humans?

Woodpeckers! Scientists study the complex skulls of wood-peckers for clues on ways to improve helmets that protect our heads. Woodpeckers strike trees on average 1,200 times a day. They do so at a speed of about fourteen miles per hour. Yet amazingly, they never sustain injury. Four components help them avoid concussions. Wood-pecker's tongues stretch around their skull and are supported by an elastic layer. They have flexible beaks. A spongy bone separates their beaks from their brains. And a fluid-filled space between their brains and skulls reduces vibrations. Industrial designers try to mimic wood-pecker's designs in making safer helmets.

DID YOU KNOW?

How to Tell the Difference between a Squirrel and a Chipmunk?

It's easy, really. Chipmunks have stripes on their faces and squirrels do not. The Townsend's chipmunk is a common mammal in Forest Park and Portland Audubon, and very vocal too, often heard chattering near the trails. Native to western Oregon and Washington forests, this chipmunk has a tell-tale sign, making it easy to differentiate among chipmunks. When it darts through the forest, it always holds its tail up like a flag!

JAY TRAIL BEGINS at the Portland Audubon Interpretive Center. After leaving the parking area, it gently descends towards Balch Creek. While walking along the pathway, listen for birdsongs that change each season of the year. Varied thrushes, Steller's jays, chestnut-backed chickadees, Pacific wrens, Anna's hummingbirds, Wilson's warblers, red-breasted nuthatches, robins, Cassin's vireos, song sparrows, and many more can be heard and observed as Jay Trail winds through green understories of salal, sword ferns, lady ferns, and thimbleberries.

At the bottom of the trail, cross Balch Creek on a bridge. Turn left and continue on Jay Trail as it passes by a pond, currently under restoration. The trail continues uphill, curving around sanctuary borders and crossing more bridges.

Along the way, think for a moment about the great work achieved by Portland Audubon in protecting Oregon's wildlife and wild landscape.

Established in 1902, the Portland chapter of the Audubon Society was among the first in the United States. It has helped establish several Oregon wildlife refuges, including Malheur, Klamath, and Three Arch Rocks. It has advocated for the creation of national forests and led campaigns for bird protection laws. In the 1930s, Portland Audubon created the first formal wildlife rehabilitation program in the United States! Currently, the Wildlife Care Center is in the process of an exciting, new expansion that will include a new surgical suite and expanded interpretive displays. Portland Audubon continues its important conservation work today and offers numerous environmental education programs throughout the year to help people learn about and connect with the natural world.

Continue walking on Jay Trail. After a half mile, the trail leads to an inspiring stand of old-growth Douglas-fir trees. A viewing deck surrounds an outstanding example of a straight-trunked, towering tree, known colloquially as the "Grandfather Tree." There is a new bench for sitting where one can look up and gaze at such a beautiful and immense life-form. Jay Trail then continues downhill, ending at a fork with Woodpecker Trail.

Turn left onto Woodpecker Trail. After a short section, it ends at a junction with lower Jay Trail. Turn left on Jay Trail. Shortly after this intersection, it is worth a side trip onto Creek Trail—a dead-end hike along the shore of lovely Balch Creek, with benches for pausing and a view into Forest Park.

Return to Jay Trail and climb uphill. The hike ends where it began, at Portland Audubon Interpretive Center and Nature Store—a wonderful place where you can find scores of terrific books on wildlife and birds and shop for bird feeders and binoculars to help deepen your exploration!

HIKE 14
Maple Trail and Wildwood Trail Loop

DISTANCE: 8.2 miles round trip. (Can be broken up into smaller trips.)
HIKING TIME: 4.5 hours
DIFFICULTY RATING: Moderate
WATERSHED: Saltzman Creek Watershed; Doane Creek Watershed
TRAILHEAD: Lower Saltzman Road

Foot traffic only on Maple Trail and Wildwood Trail. Saltzman Road and Leif Erikson Drive are also open to bicycles and horses.

MILEAGE AND DIRECTIONS
0.0   Begin at Lower Saltzman Road Trailhead off Highway 30. Hike Saltzman Road.
0.5   At intersection with Maple Trail, turn left on Maple Trail.
1.0   Cross Firelane 4. Stay on Maple Trail.
1.6   Cross Koenig Trail. Stay on Maple Trail.
2.0   Cross Leif Erikson Drive. Stay left to continue on Maple Trail, not Firelane 3.
2.3   Tie Trail to Wildwood. Stay on Maple Trail.
2.8   Maple Trail intersects Wildwood Trail. Turn right on Wildwood.
3.6   Firelane 3 intersection. Stay on Wildwood.
5.4   Intersection with Cleator Trail. Stay on Wildwood.
5.9   Wildwood intersects Saltzman Road. Turn right on Saltzman Road.
6.4   Turn left on Leif Erikson.
6.6   Turn right on Maple Trail.
7.7   Turn left on Saltzman Road.
8.2   Hike ends at Lower Saltzman Road Trailhead.

Maple Trail is one of the most scenic and serene of all pathways in Forest Park. Its glory is especially apparent in fall when its abundance of bigleaf maples shimmers with yellow highlights against the dark green of the tall, straight firs and hemlocks. As it follows Munger Creek, one enters a beautiful valley of old-growth tree specimens. This combination of Maple and Wildwood Trails offers some of the finest woodland hiking experiences in all of Forest Park.

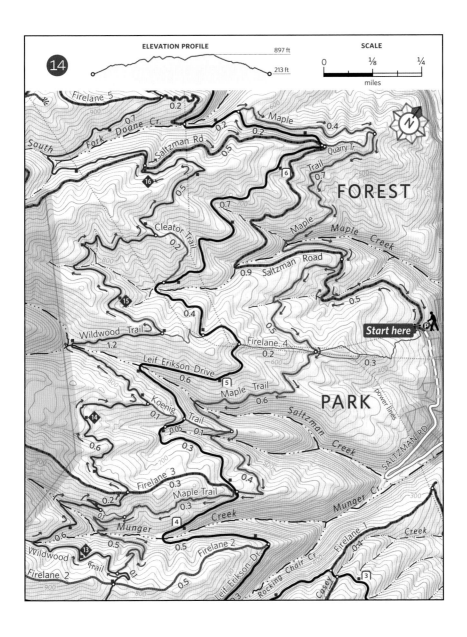

ELEVATION PROFILE

897 ft

213 ft

SCALE

0   ⅛   ¼

miles

Firelane 5

0.2

0.7

Fork Doane Cr.

Saltzman Rd

0.2

Maple

0.4

0.5

Quarry Tr.

South

16

Cleator Trail

0.5

0.2

0.7

0.7

Trail

0.7

FOREST

Maple

Maple   Creek

6

0.9   Saltzman Road

15

0.5

0.4

0.5

Start here

Wildwood Trail

1.2

Firelane 4

0.2

0.3

Leif Erikson Drive

0.6

5

Maple Trail

0.6

PARK

Saltzman

Koenig

0.1

14

Trail

0.05   0.1

0.6

0.3

0.3

Creek

power lines

SALTZMAN RD

Firelane 3

0.4

Maple Trail

0.3

Munger   Cr.

Creek

0.2

0.3

300

0.1

4

Munger   Creek

0.6

0.5

0.5

Firelane 1

0.4

13

Wildwood

0.5

Firelane 2

0.5

Rocking Chair Cr.

Casey

3

Firelane 2

Trail

0.1

Leif Erikson Dr.

0.5

0.3

CAN YOU HEAR?
The Tiny Bird with the Biggest Voice

Listen to the forest, and what do you hear? Sometimes, especially in winter and early spring, you may only hear one bird singing. But what a song! The Pacific wren—the size of a golf ball—can sing forever, it seems, without taking a breath. Its cheery song, which can last ten seconds, is high, melodic, and clear, and a hallmark of western Oregon and Washington forests. How does it accomplish such long-winded music? Because unlike  humans, who have one voice box, the larynx, these birds have two (called syrinxes), one for each side of their lungs!

CAN YOU FIND?
Forest Park's Most Common Breeding Warbler

Warblers flock to Forest Park in spring and summer; some stay to nest in the park. The most common one is the jaunty Wilson's warbler, which is also the most noticeable, for both its sweet song and striking appear-

ance. Its high-pitched notes sound like a series of jeweled "chips" running rapidly one after another, coming from branches of the fir trees. When lucky enough to see one, it's easy to identify. It's the only small, bright yellow warbler that has striking black cap on the top of its head . . . a bird wearing a black beret!

CAN YOU FIND?

Two Friendly Birds: One That Goes Up While the Other Goes Down

Two trademark bird species of Douglas-fir forest ecosystems thrive in Forest Park: the red-breasted nuthatch and brown creeper. Both may be easy to overlook, as they are small, gray or brown, but they can be spotted climbing and foraging along the trunks of trees, often occurring together. From a distance, though, what is the trick birders use to tell them apart? It's quite simple. Red-breasted nuthatches climb down tree trucks. Brown creepers climb up!

CAN YOU FIND?

A Bird Best Spotted by Its Tail

What's that rustling in the shrubs and flitting near the ground? Another small, gray bird, but hard to pinpoint? You can take a guess and probably will be right! See if you can spot white outer tail feathers flashing as they dart and hop. If you can, it's a dark-eyed junco, one of the most common native birds in Forest Park and in Douglas-fir forests of the West.

BEGIN THE HIKE by walking a half mile up Saltzman Road. From the gate on, the road is closed to all motorized traffic except park and emergency vehicles. To the right (north) notice steep Maple Creek Canyon, which is part of Doane Creek Watershed. Maple Creek, far below, drains eventually into Doane Lake, east of US Highway 30. At the intersection of Saltzman Road with Maple Trail, turn left onto the southern portion of Maple Trail.

At first, Maple Trail heads gradually uphill. Soon it begins to level out and wanders among spacious, open groves of red alder and bigleaf maples with an understory dominated by low-growing sword ferns. Listen for Pacific wrens, rufous-sided towhees, song sparrows, and a variety of woodpeckers.

Maple Trail crosses Firelane 4 after a half mile and passes underneath transmission powerlines. Keep an eye out for native Anna's and rufous hummingbirds that in spring seek the bright blooms of red-flowering currant bushes. Soon the trail enters one of the loveliest sections of central Forest Park and introduces the hiker to the rugged Saltzman Creek Watershed. The narrow woodland path drops down into a pristine canyon of cedar and hemlock and crosses Saltzman Creek on a footbridge, where verdant mosses drape from the trees and sprightly Oregon oxalis plants cover the forest floor like green shamrocks. Eventually, groves of cedars and hemlocks blend into maples, and the footpath becomes more open, with thick understories of sword fern, Oregon grape, salal, thimbleberry, and red elderberry shrubs.

At two miles, Maple Trail intersects Leif Erikson Drive. Cross Leif Erikson and continue uphill on Maple Trail. Here, the trail follows Munger Creek, named after Thornton Munger (1883–1975), a pioneering scientist who for many years was chief of research for the US Forest Service at the Pacific Northwest Experiment Station. Munger was well known for his long-term studies of native plants and wildlife of Oregon and Washington, and one of the major founders of Forest Park.

A tie trail (a sign reads "To Wildwood Trail") intersects Maple Trail at 2.3 miles. If desiring a shorter route, and one that avoids the most strenuous aspect of this hike, turn right here. Otherwise, continue on Maple Trail as it winds down picturesque Munger Creek Canyon and crosses Munger Creek—a tributary of Saltzman Creek. Maple Trail joins Wildwood Trail just before Wildwood Milepost 13. Turn right (north) onto Wildwood. For the next half mile, the trail winds in and out of an exceptionally lovely canyon of conifers, while crossing north and south tributaries of Munger Creek.

Munger Creek Canyon displays some of the largest and oldest trees in Forest Park. This is a beautiful spot for a sanctuary pause.

For three miles along Wildwood Trail, numerous native birds can often be spotted or heard at different times of the year, including western tanagers, northern pygmy owls, red-breasted nuthatches, Pacific wrens, chestnut-backed chickadees, golden-crowned kinglets, and ravens.

At Milepost 16, the trail drops down to intersect NW Saltzman Road. Leave Wildwood Trail at this point and turn right onto Saltzman Road. Stay on the road for a half mile until its intersection with Leif Erikson Drive. At the junction, turn left sharply onto Leif Erikson Drive, and head downhill. Continue north on Leif Erikson for a quarter mile until a sign demarcates Maple Trail. Turn right on Maple Trail.

This northernmost section of the pathway is shady and picturesque, overhung by draping western hemlock trees. After a mile, the trail crosses a bridge over the main stem of Maple Creek. The trail then rises out of the canyon and again intersects Saltzman Road. Turn left on Saltzman and head downhill for a half mile to reach the trailhead, completing the loop.

Great Hikes to Get to Know Your Ecosystem

HIKE 15: Understanding Watersheds
Linnton Trail and Firelane 10 Loop

DISTANCE: 3.5 miles
HIKING TIME: 2.5 hours
DIFFICULTY RATING: Moderate
WATERSHED: Linnton Creek Watershed
TRAILHEAD: Linnton Trailhead

Foot traffic only on Linnton Trail, Wildwood Trail, and Cannon Trail.
Firelane 10 is also open to bicycles and horses.

MILEAGE AND DIRECTIONS
0.0   Begin at Linnton Trailhead on US Highway 30. Hike Linnton Trail.
0.5   Intersect Firelane 10. Turn right and ascend.
0.9   Intersect Keyser Trail. Turn left onto Keyser Trail.
1.2   Intersect Firelane 10. Turn left onto Firelane 10.
1.3   Intersect Wildwood Trail. Turn left onto Wildwood Trail.
2.0   Intersect Germantown Road. Cross. Turn left onto Cannon Trail and
      descend.
2.3   Intersect Leif Erickson Parking. Cross Germantown Road. Walk uphill
      to Firelane 10.
2.4   Turn right on Firelane 10 and descend.
3.0   Intersect Linnton Trail. Turn right onto Linnton Trail.
3.5   Return to Linnton Trailhead.

Watersheds, old-growth trees, owls, salamanders, the fragrance of cedar, draping moss, even a small waterfall . . . this hike takes an explorer to the wonders
of Forest Park. As well, it reveals an important fact about ecosystems: they
are a complex community of species, habitats, and environmental conditions
that work together to function as an integrated system. Because of its size
and good condition, Linnton Creek Watershed plays an important role in
improving the health of the Willamette River by contributing clean, nutrient-
rich, aerated water to the river far below. Linnton Trail by itself can be a fun
family excursion; the entire loop exposes hikers to the scope and features of a
beautiful, intact watershed.

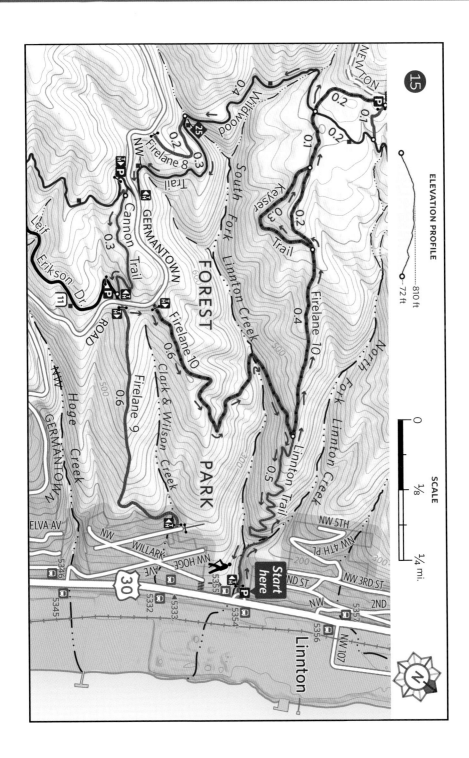

15

ELEVATION PROFILE

810 ft

72 ft

SCALE

0   ⅛   ¼ mi.

N

NEWTON

0.2
0.1
0.2
0.1

P

0.4   Wildwood

0.25

0.2
0.3

Firelane 8
NW

Trail

South Fork Linnton Creek

0.3   Keyser Trail

0.2

0.1

P

Leif Erikson Dr

Cannon Trail

0.3

GERMANTOWN

P

Firelane 10

0.6

0.4   Firelane 10

North Fork Linnton Creek

FOREST

600

500

ROAD

NW   Hoge   Creek

500

0.6   Firelane 9

Clark & Wilson Creek

PARK

300

0.5

Linnton Trail

400

ELVA AV

NW   WILLARK

NW HOGE AVE

5216

5345

30

5332

5333

5354

5355

Start here

P

NW 2ND ST

NW 5TH

NW 4TH PL

NW 3RD ST

NW

2ND

5351

5356

NW 107

300

200

GERMANTOWN

Linnton

159

DID YOU KNOW?

What Are Some of Earth's Oldest Living Things That Can Be Found Growing in Forest Park?

Western red cedars! Like Douglas-fir and western hemlock trees, these trees are evergreen and grow in older, shady forests in western Oregon and Washington. Although the ones in Forest Park are not ancient, western red cedars can reach hundreds, even thousands of years old.

Look around you. How many can you count on Linnton Trail? A good way to identify them is to look at their green leaves. Turn the leaf over! Look at the undersides of the needles. The whitish bloom of their scales looks like little butterflies!

DID YOU KNOW?

An Owl by Another Clock

While most owls are strictly nocturnal, a small, elusive native owl species lives in Forest Park and is active—*during the day*! The northern pygmy owl is surprisingly common in the park. It prefers nesting in older, large western red cedar trees growing near streams. If you listen closely while walking, you might hear its characteristic call, a repetitive single or double coo-hoot.

DID YOU KNOW?

How Can a Stream Vanish and Where Did It Go?

Streams don't really vanish; they perco-late! Creeks like those in Forest Park that aren't connected to a constant water sup-ply or a snowpack can seasonally dry up in summer when there is scant precipita-tion. What water remains infiltrates the soil and descends into the subsurface. It begins a deeper layer of movement—called an "interflow"—where it flows laterally in the "vadose zone," above the permanent water table, or groundwater. The water in these streams can resurface when precipitation resumes.

DID YOU KNOW?

What Part of the Forest Ecosystem Acts Like a Water Reservoir?

Native mosses! Like this Oregon beaked moss, these plants can hold large quantities of water. When rain falls, they ensure it drips slowly into the underlying ground, rather than all at once, in flashy flows. Moreover,

mosses purify the water in the pro-cess, keeping it cool. They help maintain moisture for all the other inhabitants of the forest. In this way, mosses con-tribute greatly to the overall health of the forest.

BEGIN THE HIKE at the Linnton Trailhead. The trail winds uphill, following Linnton Creek. Before long, city noises and sounds of traffic drop away. At the confluence of the north and south forks of Linnton Creek, a waterfall graces the trail during the wet parts of the year. Just beyond, a rustic bridge crosses North Fork Linnton Creek. Scores of maidenhair fern, hills of sword fern, and even Pacific yew trees enrich the trail.

Climbing farther, as the trail rises to the intersection towards Firelane 10, a beautiful grove of magnificent western red cedar trees awaits. This impressive tree is a hallmark of Douglas-fir forests. It was used extensively by Indigenous peoples for a variety of purposes and is prized more than nearly any other tree. Wood from it was used as material for their shelters and trees made into dugout canoes. Its fibrous bark could be shredded so finely that it could be woven into fishing nets, baskets, sails, and even into blankets and the clothes they wore.

Linnton Trail ends at a junction with Firelane 10. Continue to the right, uphill, on the fire lane, moderately steep at times. Firelane 10 is the dividing line between South and North Fork Linnton Creeks. After a half mile, turn left onto Keyser Trail. This quarter-mile side trail is named for C. Paul Keyser, who was superintendent of Portland Parks for thirty-two years, from 1917 to 1949, and thoroughly embraced the idea of creating a wilderness park along the Tualatin Mountain Range. Keyser Trail allows beautiful views into the deep canyon of South Fork Linnton Creek and is a good sanctuary pause.

Seeing the expanse along this section gives an opportunity to contemplate the breadth and scope of watersheds. Rivers, wetlands, and upland areas are connected by the seam of water. Flowing water is more than just a river between two banks. It links the upstream lands it drains, the aquifers it recharges, and the floodplain areas it periodically inundates. It reflects all the surfaces through which water courses before ever reaching the stream. Because of the extensive protection provided by Forest Park, hydrologists have determined that its watersheds are the healthiest and least altered within the city when compared with their historical conditions.

Continue on Keyser Trail until its intersection with Firelane 10. Turn left. The fire lane soon intersects Wildwood Trail. Turn left (south) onto Wildwood Trail and hike to Germantown Road. Numerous birds can often be heard on this section of trail. Upon reaching the highway, turn right, staying close to the fence to avoid busy traffic, and walk 200 feet towards the Wildwood Trail Parking Area. Cross Germantown Road here and descend on Cannon Trail.

Cannon Trail acts as a connector between Wildwood Trail and Leif Erikson parking lots. Hike Cannon Trail until the Leif Erikson Parking Area on Germantown Road. Here, cross Germantown Road once more, turn left, head uphill for 400 feet, keeping a lookout for the gate to the continuation of Firelane 10. Pass around the entry gate and descend Firelane 10.

This beautiful pathway leads to a crossing of South Fork Linnton Creek and is one of the most serene settings in Forest Park. Bald eagles can often be seen flying above the forested canyon.

At 855 acres, the Linnton Creek watershed shows high resource values and function. Like other watersheds in Forest Park, these sites warrant protection. This fact is well recognized in the 2005 Portland Watershed Management Plan: "Even at their best, technological solutions cannot replace the functions provided by habitats and species that have evolved together over millennia to create diverse, resilient, productive ecosystems. . . . Native species have a reasonable chance of survival with the right hydrology, the right habitats, adequate water quality, and biological diversity. With these elements functioning properly, the ecosystem itself is likely to become more diverse, complex, resilient, and self- sustaining."

After a half mile, Firelane 10 intersects Linnton Trail once more. Turn right and continue to the trailhead on US Highway 30, completing the loop.

HIKE 16: Understanding Wildlife Corridors
Firelane 15, Firelane 12, Wildwood Trail, and Kielhorn Trail Loop

DISTANCE: 4.5 miles
HIKING TIME: 2–2.5 hours
DIFFICULTY RATING: Moderate
WATERSHED: Miller Creek Watershed
TRAILHEAD: Firelane 15

Foot traffic only on Wildwood Trail and Kielhorn Meadow Trail.
Firelane 15, Firelane 12, and BPA Road also allow bicycles and horses.

MILEAGE AND DIRECTIONS
0.0   Begin at Firelane 15 Trailhead on NW Skyline Boulevard. Hike
      Firelane 15.
1.0   Cross Wildwood Trail. Stay on Firelane 15.
1.4   Turn right onto Firelane 12
1.9   Turn right on BPA Road.
2.2   Turn right on Wildwood Trail.
3.1   Turn left on Firelane 15.
3.4   Turn left on Kielhorn Meadow Trail and continue to end. Return to
      Firelane 15.
3.8   Turn left on Firelane 15.
4.5   End at Firelane 15 Trailhead.

These little-traveled, northernmost trails in Forest Park provide the best
chance to see wildlife rarely observed near a major city. Their distance from
the city and from population concentrations allows native animals—black-
tailed deer, elk, coyote, red-tailed hawks, bobcat, pileated woodpeckers,
pygmy owls, and even an occasional bald eagle—the opportunity to move
more freely and openly, and greatly rewards the quiet, patient observer who
spies them. In addition, from this vantage point, one can see glimpses of the
natural link between Forest Park and the habitat of the Oregon Coast Range,
commonly known as the "wildlife corridor" that permits native mammals and
birds to wander in and out of the park from more rural reservoirs.

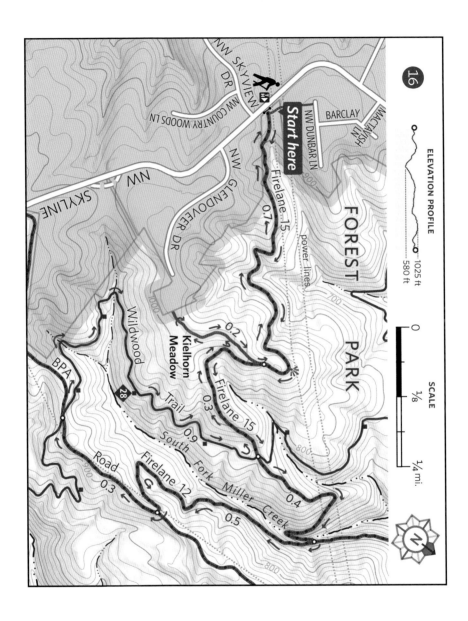

DID YOU KNOW?

How Many Bird Species Recorded by Lewis and Clark in 1806 Can Still Be Seen in Forest Park Today?

Astoundingly, nearly all of them! In his journal, William Clark wrote, "We observe the marten, small geese, the small speckled woodpecker with a white back [downy woodpecker], the blue-crested corvus [Steller's jay] ravens, crows, eagles, vultures, and hawks." This is not a random collection. Rather, it shows the relationship between wildlife that has evolved over centuries of time in native Douglas-fir habitat.

DID YOU KNOW?

Three Rock Monuments Tell the Story of a Major Development . . . That Never Happened.

Look around you and imagine if the forest were gone. It nearly was! At the confluence of Firelane 12 and BPA Road, seventy-three acres were privately owned, and twenty-five years ago were primed to be a massive housing development. Deeply alarmed, dozens of concerned citizens, in cooperation with Friends of Forest Park, Metro, and Portland Parks and Recreation, worked fervently to raise money to purchase the property. In 1999, the "Hole in the Park" was at last acquired, protected,

and donated to the city. Engraved rocks list the donors who contributed their time and money to save this critical area.

DID YOU KNOW?
It Takes a Community to Shuttle a Frog

The northern red-legged frog, at 2.5 inches long, is the largest native frog in the Pacific Northwest. Its numbers declining, it is listed as a vulnerable species by the US Fish and Wildlife Service. The largest population of these frogs in Portland occurs in Forest Park! Unfortunately, there are very few ponds in the park where the frogs can breed, and in order to reach nearby wetlands, they must cross busy US Highway 30 at the north end of the park. For years, during breeding season, frogs were getting squished trying to cross the road. Then, a community came to the rescue. Over a hundred volunteers organized. Next, Multnomah County, Oregon Department of Transportation, Oregon Department of Fish and Wildlife, and West Multnomah Soil and Water Conservation District all got on board. Now, from December to March, volunteers capture the frogs each night, place them in special buckets, and shuttle them across the road to their breeding grounds. Then, they help them return to the forest after they lay their eggs. Today, 2,000 frogs are saved each year! Currently, these same partners are also investigating possible long-term solutions, including building more breeding ponds on the Forest Park side of US Highway 30.

BEGIN HIKING FIRELANE 15 as it descends, levels off, drops again, then climbs through a variety of younger fir trees. All the fire lanes and trails along this loop lie within the beautiful Miller Creek Watershed. At several spots, Firelane 15 reveals scenic views of the Columbia River, Sauvies Island, Mt. Rainier, Mt. St. Helens, and the corridor of forest land connecting Forest Park's northwestern boundary with the rural habitat of the Coast Range.

This corridor, presently free from urbanization, is a primary reason for Forest Park's wildlife diversity. It allows easy access of native birds and mammals from other species pools into Forest Park. In fact, the future capacity of Forest Park to support wildlife will largely be determined by the park's boundary conditions. If this corridor of natural habitat is cut off from Forest Park, making the park an island surrounded on all sides by urban growth and fragmentation, the capability of the park to sustain a diversity of wildlife and plant species will be dramatically reduced.

Stay on Firelane 15 until it ends at an intersection with Firelane 12. Interesting birds can often be seen and heard along these fire lanes. Red-tailed hawks, common ravens, and turkey vultures can be observed flying above the treetops. Ruby-crowned and golden-crowned kinglets call from perches hidden in the forest. Varied thrushes, becoming more rare each year, can be heard singing near South Fork Miller Creek.

At the intersection of Firelanes 15 and 12, turn right and continue uphill on the upper portion of Firelane 12. In spring, this path is abloom with trilliums. After a half mile, Firelane 12 ends and joins BPA Road. Turn right and continue hiking uphill on BPA Road for a quarter mile. At the road's intersection with Wildwood Trail, turn right again onto Wildwood.

Hike north for one mile, following South Fork Miller Creek and passing through groves of western red cedar. This section of Wildwood Trail crosses seven bridges and winds close to the headwaters of Miller Creek, while offering glimpses into beautiful, deep Miller Creek Canyon. After Mile 28¼, Wildwood Trail comes out at Firelane 15. Turn left on Firelane 15.

In a quarter mile, Firelane 15 intersects with Kielhorn Meadow Trail. To visit the meadow, a tranquil forest clearing, turn left for a quarter mile more. As there is no exit to Skyline Boulevard from here, conclude the hike by returning to Firelane 15. Turn left and hike up the fire lane to return to the trailhead.

HIKE 17: Understanding Interior Forest Habitat
Wildwood Trail: From Newberry Road to Firelane 15

DISTANCE: 3.5 miles
HIKING TIME: 2 hours
DIFFICULTY RATING: Easy
WATERSHED: Miller Creek Watershed
TRAILHEAD: Newberry Road

Foot traffic only.

MILEAGE AND DIRECTIONS
0.0   Begin at Newberry Road Trailhead. Hike south on Wildwood Trail.
1.8   Intersection of Firelane 15. Return north on Wildwood Trail.
3.6   End at Newberry Road Trailhead.

The final section of Wildwood Trail takes a hiker into the less-traveled North Unit of Forest Park. This part of the park features fine interior forest habitat—native landscape that is whole, contiguous, and unfragmented by roadways, clear cuts, or development. As such, it provides important wildlife habitat for many native species. This habitat is extremely rare in the Portland area. Moreover, Miller Creek—which this trail will cross on ten different bridges—is one of the most valued streams in Portland. Traveling through these natural areas among the tall trees and healthy streams, the full majesty of Forest Park becomes clear. Here, it is easy to see why Forest Park is considered to be the "crown jewel" of Portland's park system.

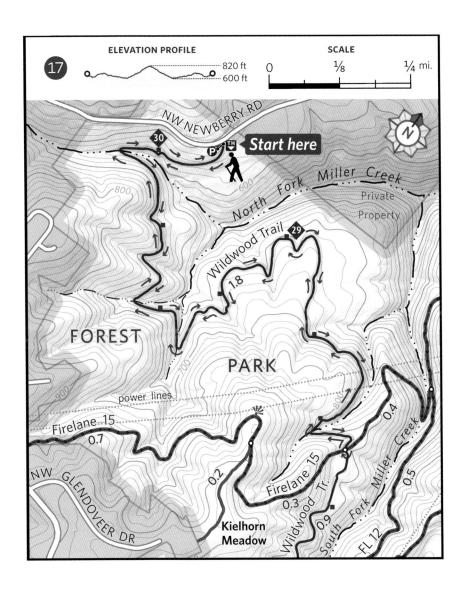

ELEVATION PROFILE

17   820 ft
      600 ft

SCALE

0   ⅛   ¼ mi.

NW NEWBERRY RD

30

TH
Start here

P

600

North Fork Miller Creek

Private Property

800

Wildwood Trail

29

1.8

FOREST

PARK

700

900

power lines

800

Firelane 15

0.7

0.4

0.2

Firelane 15

0.3

South Fork Miller Creek

0.5

NW GLENDOVEER DR

Kielhorn Meadow

Wildwood Tr.

0.9

FL 12

DID YOU KNOW?
When Is Decay NOT Decay?

When it's a snag! A snag is defined as a standing dead tree, at least four inches wide at chest height and six feet tall. It may look decrepit, but a snag plays an important role in the forest. Instead of thinking of it as "decay," wildlife biologists consider it "life giving" to many species of birds and mammals. Snags are essential for cavity-nesting birds such as woodpeckers to live in. And when snags deteriorate, the insects within them provide food for many animals.

DID YOU KNOW?
Fallen Trees: The Best Recyclers

Forest Park has lots of downed logs scattered in its woods— timber felled by windstorms and age. But a tree's importance doesn't end just because it has died and fallen. Far from it! As the logs decay, they enhance the soil and assist in nutrient cycling. Fungi recycle minerals in the dead timber and transfigure it into a form that can be reclaimed by live trees to help them grow!

DID YOU KNOW?

Old-Growth: Cellulose Cemetery or Important Natural Reservoir?

Researchers have discovered that old-growth forests are far from being decadent habitats. Instead, they make up a complex ecosystem and play a critical role in forest health. Older forests are important carbon sinks, absorbing carbon and mitigating climate change. Giant trees hold within them rich gene pools that contain characteristics such as longevity and the ability to ward off disease. These traits are vital for the welfare and stability of future generations of trees. Long live old-growth!

DID YOU KNOW?

How Many of Forest Park Birds Are Listed as "Special Status Species"?

One third! At least thirty-six species of birds in Forest Park are Special Status Species. While many remain common in the park, they are significantly declining in the region and some across all of Oregon. Such reductions of native bird species are becoming common throughout the nation. Even more worrisome, over the past fifty years, scientists have determined we have lost over 3 billion birds in North America.

That is one reason why the Forest Park Management Plan specifies that the protection of wildlife communities is a primary goal for the park.

BEGIN THE HIKE at the Newberry Road Trailhead. Walk south on this final section of 30-mile Wildwood Trail, the longest natural woodland trail winding through a city park anywhere in the United States. The trail lies entirely within the Miller Creek Watershed and crosses both the North and South Forks of Miller Creek several times. The Miller Creek Watershed exhibits some of the best health in all of Forest Park. Its vitality is the result of the excellent quality of much of its native vegetation and the fact that its headwaters are predominantly intact; only a few small pockets of private development occur in its upper basins. Miller Creek is one of only two streams in Forest Park (the other being Balch Creek) known to support fish. It contains small but essential populations of sea-run cutthroat trout, steelhead, and Coho salmon. Remarkably, considering this is a creek within city limits, recent studies show Miller Creek's quality is comparable to some of the best and healthiest streams in western Oregon.

For the first mile, the trail winds in and out of deep coniferous woods. At Milepost 29½, it enters a beautiful cedar grove where a careful observer might hear a rare varied thrush or the wild call of a pileated woodpecker. These species, along with band-tailed pigeons, olive-sided flycatchers, western wood pewees, and many others, are suffering declines. In fact, 30 percent of the native birds and mammals in Forest Park are designated as Special Status Species and are prioritized for conservation.

Continuing south, Wildwood Trail passes by widely spaced, tall cedar and hemlock trees that grow among stately maple and red alder. Expansive carpets of sword ferns cover the forest floor. Throughout this stretch near Milepost 29, pileated woodpeckers—referred to by many bird-watchers are "the Spirit of the Northwest"—are frequently observed and heard drumming. A quarter mile farther, the trail passes many old stumps of trees, revealing its past logging history. Springboard notches, cut by loggers long ago, can still be seen on some of the large stumps. Western red cedar is making a comeback, though, growing among stands of bigleaf maple trees.

The tenth bridge along the trail occurs shortly before Firelane 15 and crosses South Fork Miller Creek. Looking to the north reveals exceptionally lovely views of Miller Creek Canyon, where the stream is making its way towards the Willamette River. Of all rivers in Forest Park, only Miller Creek is not culverted to its confluence with the Willamette. It remains one of the last free-flowing waterways in the city of Portland.

Wildwood Trail intersects Firelane 15 just before Milepost 28¼. For the return trip, retrace your steps.

Great Hikes for Getting in Shape

HIKE 18
BPA Road, Newton Road, and Wildwood Trail Loop

DISTANCE: 5 miles
HIKING TIME: 3 hours
DIFFICULTY RATING: Strenuous
WATERSHED: Miller Creek Watershed; Newton Creek Watershed
TRAILHEAD: BPA Road/NW Skyline Boulevard

Foot traffic only on Wildwood Trail. BPA Road and Newton Road also allow both bicycles and horses.

MILEAGE AND DIRECTIONS
0.0   Begin hike at BPA Road Trailhead on Skyline Boulevard.
0.5   Intersection with Wildwood Trail. Stay on BPA Road.
0.8   Intersection with Firelane 12. Stay on BPA Road.
1.2   Intersection with Firelane 13. Stay on BPA Road.
2.1   Junction near US Highway 30. Turn right onto Newton Road.
3.4   Newton Road intersects Wildwood Trail. Turn right on Wildwood.
4.5   Turn left on BPA Road.
5.0   End at BPA Road Trailhead.

Of all the hiking trails in Forest Park, this loop is one of the most diverse as it ranges from one of the highest points of the park along Skyline Boulevard to descend 1,000 feet to US Highway 30 (NW St. Helens Road). While steep footing in places, this hike rewards the walker with outstanding views of mountains and rivers and glimpses of the wildlife corridor to the north. BPA Road is the dividing line between two of the healthiest watersheds in the entire Portland park system: Miller Creek and Newton Creek Watersheds.

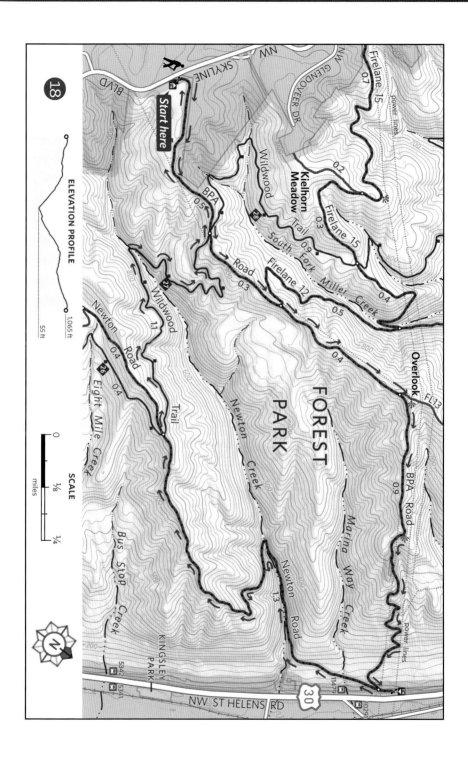

CAN YOU FIND?
The Smallest Birds of Forest Park

Hummingbirds are the smallest migrating birds in North America. Anna's and rufous hummingbirds nest in Forest Park, and measure only 3.5 inches, more like a large moth! Rufous hummingbirds are primarily reddish orange in color while Anna's are green with a red throat. These natives are so small that their average weight is no more than a nickel. Their hearts can beat as fast as 1,260 beats per minute and their wings between twelve to eighty beats per second. During migration, they can travel up to 500 miles at a time.

DID YOU KNOW?
What Is One Thing That Hummingbirds Can Do That No Other Bird Can?

Hummingbirds can fly backward!

DID YOU KNOW?

What Forest Park Organisms Are Widely Used to Study the Quality of the Air We Breathe?

Lichens! These remarkable nonflowering organisms do not have stems, leaves, or roots to survive. Rather, they absorb their nutrients from the air. In doing so, they also take in any air pollutants that might exist. Lichens grow exceptionally well in areas with clean air but will die if sulfur dioxide levels rise too high. Scientists now look to lichens as an important partner to help monitor air quality.

DID YOU KNOW?

What's So Special about Red Alder?

In spring, look for the trees that transform the woods with a blush of rosy pink. Besides lovely to look at, these red alder trees are performing work that benefits the forest. They have the rare ability to "fix" nitrogen directly from the air—converting it into a form they can use for their growth and, at the same, time, release it into the soil. This valuable function can help restore soil nutrients in areas where they have been depleted as a result of logging or fire.

BEGIN THE HIKE on Bonneville Power Administration (BPA) Road, a grassy thoroughfare that feels more like a quiet country lane than a utility access. For several years, BPA has coordinated transmission line maintenance and vegetation management with Portland Parks and Recreation, Metro, and the Xerces Society. Working together, they share a common goal to preserve Forest Park's attributes as important pollinator habitat helping to attract native bees and birds.

BPA Road starts off heading slightly uphill, traversing under maple trees and alders that arch overhead. Soon it begins a gentle descent. Along the road, outstanding views of Mt. St. Helens, Mt. Adams, and Mt. Rainier can be seen. In June, beautiful native orange tiger lilies are plentiful on the trail as well as numerous wildflowers planted to encourage pollinators. Red-tailed hawks can often be seen flying overhead.

Continue on BPA Road for two miles, ignoring all side trails. As the path approaches US Highway 30, its pitch becomes steeper. At these lower elevations along the road, look for native Oregon white oak trees, which are uncommon in Forest Park. Also be observant for poison oak, prevalent in patches nearer the highway. BPA Road ends at an orange park gate at US Highway 30. Before reaching the gate, though, there is a junction making a sharp turn to the right. This is Newton Road and the start of a scenic uphill portion of the loop.

Newton Road begins as a narrow trail. It crosses Marina Way Creek and soon begins to climb. The pathway follows picturesque Newton Creek for a quarter mile. It leads through the center of Newton Canyon, passing through luxuriant groves of cedar and hemlock and maple trees draped with moss. After one mile, Newton Road widens as it begins to rise more abruptly uphill, between Newton Creek Canyon to the north and Bus Stop Creek Canyon to the south. It is a perfect spot for a sanctuary pause. The trail levels as it nears an intersection with Wildwood Trail. At the junction, turn right onto Wildwood.

From Milepost 26¼ to 26¾, Wildwood Trail gently meanders along the walls of beautiful Newton Canyon. Superb specimens of old-growth trees can be found here, and native plants and ferns thrive—another perfect place for a sanctuary pause.

This section is one of only a few pockets in Forest Park where true old-growth features can be observed. Under natural conditions, certain traits begin to be noticeable in forest stands that are over 150 years old. These include the presence of huge trees that often have irregular crowns, or broken tops, and overtop the adjoining canopy. In Newton Canyon, some Douglas-fir giants reach up to 200 feet in height and eighty-seven inches in diameter at breast height. Other structural attributes indicative of old-growth habitat are the occurrence of large, standing dead trees (snags) and a prevalence of hefty dead and downed logs in various stages of decay. Snags are essential for cavity-nesting birds such as woodpeckers, and downed logs contribute to the health and nutrient level of the soil. Both of these features can be seen along this stretch of Wildwood Trail.

After Milepost 27, Wildwood Trail switchbacks several times and climbs up towards BPA Road. Along this section, the character of the forest vegetation changes yet again. Cedar, fir, and hemlock are reduced. The south-facing slope of Newton Canyon is predominately made up of younger maple and alder trees with a dense understory growth of elderberry, salmonberry, and other common shrubs. BPA Road intersects Wildwood Trail just before Milepost 27½ . Turn left here and complete the loop by hiking up BPA Road a half mile more to return to the parking area.

HIKE 19
Lower and Upper Ridge Trails, Springville Road, Wildwood Trail, and Hardesty Trail Loop

DISTANCE: 4.2 miles
HIKING TIME: 2.5 hours
DIFFICULTY RATING: Strenuous
WATERSHED: Springville Creek Watershed
TRAILHEAD: Lower Ridge Trail

Foot traffic only on Ridge Trail, Hardesty Trail, and Wildwood Trail. Springville Road and Leif Erikson Drive are also open to bicycles and horses. Firelane 7 is open to pedestrians and horses only.

MILEAGE AND DIRECTIONS
0.0   Begin at Ridge Trail Trailhead entrance at the west end of the St. Johns Bridge. Hike Lower Ridge Trail.
0.6   Ridge Trail intersects Leif Erikson Drive. Turn left forty yards then right on the continuation of Ridge Trail.
0.9   Continue straight ahead at the junction of Wildwood Trail. Hike Upper Ridge Trail.
1.3   Turn right at the junction with Firelane 7. Hike 0.4 miles until intersection with Springville Road.
1.7   Turn right on Springville Road. Hike to intersection with Wildwood Trail.
2.0   Turn right on Wildwood Trail. Hike until intersection with Hardesty Trail.
2.8   Turn left on Hardesty Trail. Hike until intersection with Leif Erikson Drive.
3.1   Turn right on Leif Erikson. Hike until intersection with Lower Ridge Trail.
3.6   Turn left onto Lower Ridge Trail.
4.2   End at trailhead at St. Johns Bridge.

This highly scenic loop dramatically reveals the dynamic interface of the many components that combine to give Forest Park its unique vitality. Views of bridges and industry mingle with vistas of mountains, rivers, quiet woods,

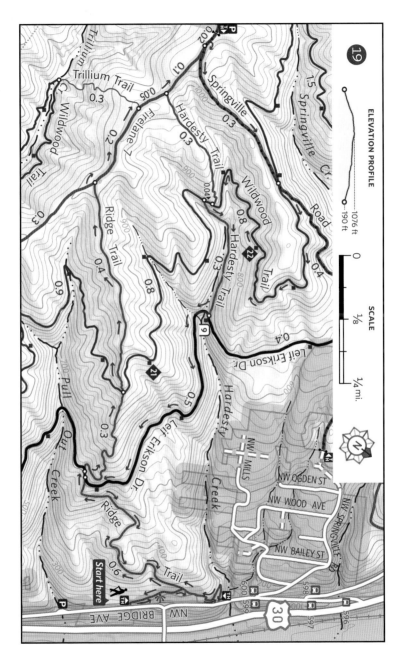

and native canyons. Together they create an unusual expression—the transformation of a cacophonous industrial setting into a sanctuary of wildness, naturalness, and beauty.

CAN YOU FIND?
A Shamrock Flower for St. Patrick's Day

If you scan some of the wettest, richest parts of the forest floor lying beneath tall Douglas-fir trees, you may find a happy plant that looks like a clover. Oregon oxalis can make what appears a shamrock carpet on the ground, topped with a pretty, white, five-petaled flower that emerges around March. Look hard enough and maybe you will find a four-leaf clover!

DID YOU KNOW?
What One Geologic Feature Possibly Saved Forest Park?

Portland Hills Silt! This upper formation, lying on top the base rock of Columbia River Basalt, is a poor foundation material. Laid down during the last million years of Pleistocene, fine textured clay silt was transported by winds to the south and west of the Columbia River's flood-

plain. It is the final capping foundation in most of the West Hills of Portland, with its greatest thickness occurring in Forest Park. When wet, it is highly unstable. The result is large areas of washout along Leif Erikson Drive, making the road and steep lands around it very difficult to develop.

DID YOU KNOW?

What Made That Big Notch in That Tree Trunk?

It was created by loggers, who cut down that tree a century ago! While working to harvest Douglas-firs, they made notches where they fitted wooden slats, called "springboards," into the gash. Old-time loggers would stand on the springboards, which were five feet long by eight inches wide, for support while they sawed down the immense trees.

CAN YOU FIND?

The Third Coniferous Tree of Forest Park That Often Gets Overlooked

Western hemlock is an important native tree of moist northwest forests. Often, however, it appears overshadowed by its more conspicuous counterparts—Douglas-fir and western red cedar, which grow more

rapidly, attain greater size, and can live much longer. Yet the western hemlock has a special advantage the others don't: it can grow steadily and healthfully in dense shade. Look at rotting logs and stumps in Forest Park to see many hemlock seedings impressively growing. And when they are taller? They can be recognized by their tops, which have a graceful, characteristic droop.

TO BEGIN THE HIKE, climb the staircase adjacent to the west end of the St. Johns Bridge.

Ridge Trail begins with a blasting of noise from nearby industry, cars, and semi-trucks. Underfoot, dense growths of ivy and other invasive plants threaten to crowd out native vegetation. But the initial path is not unpleasant: after a few hundred yards a small wooden bridge crosses the ravine, and from here there is a spectacular close-up view of the historic St. Johns Bridge, with a backdrop of Mt. St. Helens and the Willamette River.

After the crossing, the trail climbs steadily upward as it rises through Pull Out Creek Canyon. Before long, ivy declines, and the city is left behind. Climbing higher, cathedral-like firs come into view. After 0.5 miles, Ridge Trail intersects Leif Erikson Drive. Turn left on Leif Erikson for approximately forty yards to access the upper portion of Ridge Trail. Turn right and continue on Ridge Trail, which is aptly named as it climbs up the middle of two adjoining canyons. To the left (south) is Pull Out Creek Canyon; to the right (north) is Hardesty Creek Canyon. After 0.3 miles, Ridge Trail intersects Wildwood Trail. Stay straight on Ridge Trail as it begins to level out while passing among graceful archways made up of draping branches of native vine maple.

Ridge Trail intersects Firelane 7. Turn right on Firelane 7 and continue climbing uphill. Along this section of Firelane 7, be sure to keep an eye open for black-tailed deer tracks, which are especially noticeable in muddy spots in the wet seasons.

Firelane 7 ends as it joins with Springville Road. Take a sharp right onto Springville Road. Beautiful Springville Creek Canyon offers a sense of solitude. Presently, the headwaters of the Springville Creek Watershed are nearly intact and only lightly developed. This feature is significant, as it is important to preserve the headwaters within a watershed because they determine the integrity of an entire drainage system. What happens in the headwaters translates all the way down the stream. In steep drainages, such as those within Forest Park that are also short in length, entire streams can become degraded if headwaters lose their native vegetation and are developed.

At the intersection of Springville Road and Wildwood Trail, turn right onto Wildwood. When the trail is wet in winter and spring, this trail abounds with interesting varieties of luxuriant mosses and unusually shaped lichens. After nearly a mile, Wildwood Trail intersects Upper and Lower Hardesty Trail. Turn left to access the lower portion of Hardesty Trail.

Lower Hardesty Trail is tranquil, shady, and verdant as it follows Hardesty Creek. It is adorned with numerous young western hemlock trees, many growing from huge stumps acting as nurse logs. Several of the largest stumps show evidence of springboard notches, remnants of logging activities from long ago.

Hardesty Trail emerges at Leif Erikson Drive at Leif Erikson Milepost 9. Turn right (south) onto Leif Erikson next to a large road cut. On this outcropping, a sheer wall of delicate maidenhair ferns can be seen clinging to the Columbia River Basalt. After Milepost 8½, Lower Ridge Trail comes in on the left. Turn here, continue downhill, and head back towards St. Johns Bridge. The forest loop ends where the city, once again, begins.

HIKE 20
Firelane 5, Wildwood Trail, Wiregate Trail, and Cleator Trail Loop

DISTANCE: 6.6 miles
HIKING TIME: 3 hours
DIFFICULTY RATING: Strenuous
WATERSHED: Doane Creek Watershed
TRAILHEAD: Upper Saltzman Road

Foot traffic only on Wildwood Trail, Wiregate Trail, and Cleator Trail.
Leif Erikson Drive and Saltzman Road are also open to bicycles and horses.
Firelane 5 is open to pedestrians and cyclists only.

MILEAGE AND DIRECTIONS
0.0   Begin at Upper Saltzman Road Trailhead. Hike Firelane 5.
0.9   Turn left at intersection with Wildwood Trail. Hike Wildwood Trail.
2.4   Intersection with Wiregate Trail. Turn right onto Wiregate Trail.
2.7   Intersection with Leif Erikson Drive. Turn right onto Leif Erikson.
4.3   Intersection with Cleator Trail. Turn right onto Cleator Trail.
4.5   Intersection with Wildwood Trail. Turn right onto Wildwood.
5.7   Intersection with Firelane 5. Turn left onto Firelane 5.
6.6   End at Saltzman Road Trailhead.

This wonderful loop takes hikers into the lovely Central Unit of Forest Park, meandering through some of the park's more remote areas, which are particularly enjoyable for their solitude. In summer, the trails are cooling on a hot day, offering shade beneath overarching canopies of fir and vine maple trees. In spring, because of an abundance of bigleaf maple, the hike allows good birdwatching opportunities as migrating and breeding birds flock together to feed on the abundant maple catkins. As an added bonus, this section of Wildwood Trail follows peaceful Sanctuary Creek—a sparkling tributary of Doane Creek, one of Forest Park's most important streams.

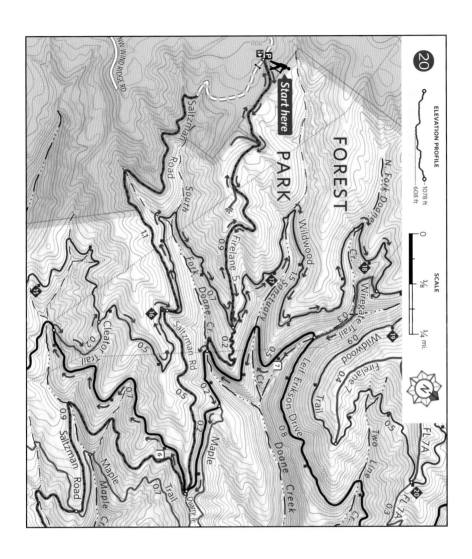

CAN YOU FIND?
Why Is That Tree Curving?

Throughout Forest Park numerous large Douglas-fir and cedar trees have an intriguing curve at their bases, making the lower parts of the trunks resemble the grip of a pistol. This phenomenon is the result of earth slides that occurred when the trees were young, forcing them in

a downhill angle. In an effort to reach out for sunlight, the young trees worked to grow upward and upright. This is a common sight in western Oregon wherever there are steep, moist ravines.

DID YOU KNOW?
The Story of the Blue Diamonds

Who invented the idea of painting blue diamonds on trees along Wildwood Trail and why? That story rests with a humble man who loved Forest Park and devoted himself to it for over sixty years: Fran Koenig. After serving in World War II, Fran discovered Forest Park. Soon, it became his passion. Fascinated by maps, he decided to measure the trails of the park. Devising an ingenious measuring wheel, he computed trail lengths of every trail. Then, he conceived of a diamond, painted blue, at quarter-mile intervals along Wildwood Trail to help with navigation. Today, Fran's 120 blue diamonds are emblematic of the world-famous Wildwood Trail.

DID YOU KNOW?

Shephard's Folly Saved Forest Park!

In 1914, land developer Richard Shephard had big plans. He hoped to sell thousands of homes platted along a scenic drive. To make that happen, he spearheaded the construction of "Hillside Drive"—an eleven-mile, country road winding 600 feet above the Willamette River, now known as Leif Erikson Drive. His goal of a massive development nearly came true—but then the rains came. Landslide after landslide occurred along the cut surfaces. No one wanted the homesites. Shephard's dream was dashed. But in its place, a park was born.

CAN YOU FIND?

Columbia River Basalt

Sixteen million years ago, fissures in southeastern Washington and northeastern Oregon spewed fluid lava, covering tens of thousands of square miles. Hardening into basalt, this is what makes up much of the underlay-

ment of Forest Park. All along the cut banks of Leif Erikson Drive, basalt exposures can be seen. A key feature: many exposures are covered with green licorice ferns that take root in the worn crevices of rock.

BEGIN THE HIKE at Firelane 5, which starts behind a locked park gate. At first, the wide pathway is mostly level before descending deeper into Doane Creek Canyon. At the intersection of Firelane 5 and Wildwood Trail, turn left (north) onto Wildwood, and remain on the trail for the next 1.5 miles.

This is an exceptionally beautiful part of Wildwood Trail that curves in and out of canyons excised by Doane Creek and its tributaries. At 1,037 acres, Doane Creek Watershed is the second largest watershed in Forest Park. It incorporates numerous side creeks that trickle down through the canyon in winter and spring. In fall, the prolific vine maple trees lining the trail make it a landscape of color. Hiking along this picturesque segment of Wildwood one follows Sanctuary Creek—appropriately named, as any part of the path is a pleasing place for a sanctuary pause.

Soon after Wildwood Milepost 18, Wiregate Trail comes in on the right. Leave Wildwood here and descend on Wiregate Trail—a quiet and scenic path at the confluence of two tributaries of Doane Creek. Sections are steep and can be slippery when wet. Wiregate Trail exits onto Leif Erickson Drive. Turn right onto Leif Erikson and hike for 1.5 miles. Good views of Columbia River Basalt, adorned with a variety of ferns and mosses, are visible in the road cuts. At Leif Erikson's intersection with Salzman Road, a wide-spanning view of the St. Johns Bridge, Vancouver Lake, and the confluence of the Willamette and Columbia Rivers can be seen when leaves are off the trees. Cross Saltzman Road and continue on Leif Erickson until its intersection with Cleator Trail, which comes in from the right.

At the junction, turn right onto Cleator Trail. The quarter-mile path is named for Fred Cleator (1884–1957), supervisor for recreation for the US Forest Service in Oregon and Washington in the early part of the twentieth century. Cleator was instrumental in the founding of Forest Park. Under his direction, he also initiated and created another treasure: the Skyline Trail, which was later incorporated into the Pacific Crest Trail.

Cleator Trail ends at its connection with Wildwood Trail. Turn right onto Wildwood and head north. After a half mile, the trail crosses South Fork Doane Creek on a large bridge. A half-mile farther, just prior to Milepost 16¾, Wildwood intersects again with Firelane 5. Turn left and head up the fire lane, returning to the parking area, to complete the loop.

HIKE 21
Lower Firelane 1, Upper Firelane 1, and Nature Trail Loop

DISTANCE: 5 miles
HIKING TIME: 2.5 hours
DIFFICULTY RATING: Strenuous
WATERSHED: Willbridge Watershed; Saltzman Creek Watershed
TRAILHEAD: Lower Firelane 1

Foot traffic only on Nature Trail.
Firelane 1 and Leif Erikson Drive also allow both horses and bicycles.

MILEAGE AND DIRECTIONS
0.0   Begin at Lower Firelane 1 Parking Area and Trailhead. Hike Lower Firelane 1.
1.5   Cross Leif Erikson Drive. Make a slight jog to the left. Continue on Upper Firelane 1.
2.0   Intersect Nature Trail. Turn sharply right onto Nature Trail.
3.0   Nature Trail intersects Leif Erikson. Turn right onto Leif Erikson.
3.4   At intersection with Lower Firelane 1, turn left.
4.9   End at Lower Firelane 1 Trailhead.

For those wishing to get in shape for summer hiking in the mountains, this loop provides good conditioning, for it climbs 900 feet in less than two miles. For the first mile, it parallels US Highway 30—the park's heavy industry boundary. While noisy with road and industry traffic, it also yields year-round, panoramic views of four mountains and the chance to explore a section of Forest Park where there are no other trails. In addition, black-tailed deer use this travel corridor, migratory birds enjoy the more open habitat, and the opportunity to spy raptors—red-tailed hawks, bald eagles, and turkey vultures—is greater here than on almost any other trail in Forest Park. Specimens of Oregon white oak, becoming rarer each year, can also be found acting as a buffer between the trail and highway.

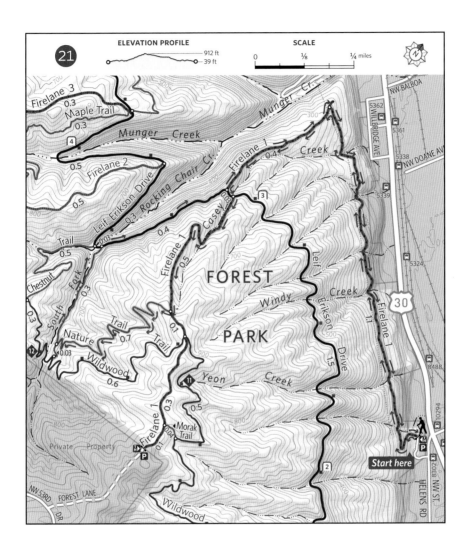

CAN YOU FIND?
A Tree Whose Bark Is Peeling

In the moist coastlines from Puget Sound to northern California and in certain spots in Forest Park you will discover an evergreen tree unlike other evergreens you may think of. It's a Pacific madrone, a "broadleaved evergreen" that boasts glossy, green, leathery leaves three to six inches long. These leaves continue growing for two years and don't fall off until a new

set has replaced them with more green leaves. The most unusual thing about this tall tree, though, is its distinctive red bark. When mature, it peels away in thin sheets, like paper!

DID YOU KNOW?
What Are Those Generous Wide Pathways in Forest Park?

Fire lanes! Fire lanes remain an integral part of Forest Park and its fire-fighting strategy. A system of eleven fire lanes was built in 1952, after the devastating "Bonny Slope Burn" in 1951 that torched over 1,200 acres in Forest Park, and even more on lands to the west. They are twelve-foot-wide roads where emergency equipment can travel in case of a fire or health emergency. Fire lanes allow critical access down and across the forested slopes of the park for fire-fighting equipment. All are open to pedestrians to explore.

DID YOU KNOW?

What Makes Those Neat Horizontal Holes on Dead Trees?

Red-breasted sapsuckers—a colorful woodpecker with a bright red head and breast and the most fastidious way of drilling of any bird. Searching for plant sap, seeds, ants, beetles, aphids, spiders, and more, the sapsucker drills perfect, small, round holes in horizontal rows, around and around a tree trunk. It shares its bounty with warblers and hummingbirds that feed on the sap and insects near its drilled holes.

CAN YOU FIND?

The "Other" Fern of Forest Park

Unlike the majority of ferns in Forest Park that favor cool, moist, shady environments, bracken ferns like sun, thrive in more open habitats, and prefer drier soils. That's why they are easier to find near fire lanes or powerline pathways in Forest Park. It is one of the most common and widespread ferns in the Pacific Northwest. They are large ferns, growing two to four feet tall, and resemble lady ferns. Bracken fern  leaves, however, don't taper like lady ferns. Rather, they have multiple branches that are triangular in shape, coming to a point at the top.

THE HIKE BEGINS from a newly constructed parking lot and rises uphill until it reaches the Portland General Electric (PGE) powerline. For the first mile, Lower Firelane 1 follows the powerline. These lower, easternmost reaches of Forest Park have an industrial feel. The vegetation along the highway is degraded with large tracts of invasive weeds, predominantly English ivy and Himalayan blackberry. Fortunately, Portland Parks and Recreation is leading a collaborative effort, with PGE, City of Portland Bureau of Environmental Services, and Portland Fire and Rescue, to clean up these degraded sites surrounding the powerline. They share a maintenance goal of keeping the fire lane passable with standards designed for access in the case of wildfire.

From the start, Lower Firelane 1 offers an undulating walk that rises and falls as it crosses numerous intermittent creeks within the Willbridge Watershed—most notably Yeon, Windy, and Casey Creeks. While noise and clamor from the industrial area is a constant companion, it is tempered and modulated with native cries of red-tailed hawks coming from overhead. In a half-mile, shortly after passing Windy Creek, wide-ranging views from this low shoulder make the trip extraordinary and definitely worth it. An overlook reveals Mt. Rainier, Mt. St. Helens, Mt. Adams, and Mt. Hood, as well as a panorama of Portland, extending from the US Bank Building ("Big Pink") downtown through the industrial area, Swan Island, University of Portland, to the Burlington and St. Johns Bridges, and beyond.

At one mile, Firelane 1 makes an abrupt ninety-degree turn to the left as it ends at a promontory directly above Rocking Chair Creek Canyon. Here it leaves the powerline, and the character of the fire lane quickly changes. The trail climbs, very steeply in parts, up a ridge that separates two watersheds— Willbridge to the south and Saltzman Creek to the north. City noise drops out, invasive vegetation is dramatically reduced, and the landscape becomes natural and beautiful. Glades of sword ferns cover the forest floor. Native red-breasted sapsuckers frequent the habitat and are commonly seen nesting. Near the intersection with Leif Erikson Drive, a scenic grove of madrone trees borders the pathway.

At the intersection, jog to the left on Leif Erikson Drive, then turn right to continue on Upper Firelane 1, gaining elevation, sometimes rapidly. The path borders scenic Casey Creek, named after Casey Puterbaugh (1986– 2018)—hiker, mountain biker, and Forest Park advocate—who loved this urban wilderness and was dedicated to defending and preserving the park's natural attributes up until the time of his death.

After a half mile, Nature Trail comes in on the right. Make a sharp turn to the right onto Nature Trail. Continue hiking as the picturesque, mile-long trail wends in and out of numerous ravines of fir and maple. At its junction with Leif Erikson Drive, turn right on the roadway. This part of Leif Erikson showcases grand views of the steepest and most impressive section of Rocking Chair Creek Canyon. Large outcroppings of basalt border the road and its walls are punctuated with abundant growths of licorice ferns.

At Leif Erikson's junction with Lower Firelane 1, turn left. Descend the fire lane and continue until its end at St. Helens Road, completing the loop.

Afterword
Forest Park: Urban Biodiversity Reserve

A half century ago, the United Nations Educational, Scientific and Cultural Organization (UNESCO) did something remarkable. In 1968, UNESCO assembled the first Biosphere Conference. The conference examined how the conservation of natural resources could be reconciled with their sustainable use by humankind. One of the projects that evolved was the idea of establishing a coordinated world network of sites representing important natural ecosystems in which genetic resources would be protected, monitored, and studied—a living laboratory. These sites, once identified, would be called "biosphere reserves." "Biosphere" refers to the land, water, and atmosphere that gives earth life. "Reserve" means that the designated area is special and protected—a place of unusual scientific and natural attributes where we find pathways toward sustainable development.

The concept grew, deepened, and expanded around the world. By 2022, 738 UNESCO Biosphere Reserves have been established worldwide in 134 countries. Their numbers continue to grow. Within the United States, numerous national parks have become biosphere reserves, including Everglades, Great Smoky Mountain, Olympic, Yellowstone, and Glacier. Currently, Oregon has only one biosphere reserve: the Cascade Head Biosphere Reserve, a 102,220-acre site on the central Oregon Coast.

Biosphere reserves are voluntary designations. They come with no standardized legal protections. In general, they act most often as a bridge for future conservation strategies, with the aim of fostering harmonious integration of people and nature. They occur where an area has great conservation value and the community surrounding it pledges to protect biodiversity and cultural heritage.

Biosphere reserves showcase the distinctiveness of an ecosystem and help create a "sense of place" among visitors. A major goal is to preserve an ecosystem's native vegetation and wildlife, and to promote management, education, and research in the realm of ecosystem conservation. They are created so that an area's natural heritage can be protected and transmitted to future generations.

The biosphere reserve program continues to expand every year, and dozens of new sites achieve the UNESCO title globally. At the time of this writing, however, entirely urban biosphere reserves have yet to be included in the list. Scientists are currently advocating for urban biosphere reserves since nearly half of the total global population lives in cities.

This is where many believe Forest Park could play a pivotal role.

With its outstanding attributes, Portland's Forest Park has the potential to be a prototype and a catalyst for an important new designation: "urban biodiversity reserve." Already, Forest Park affords many of the qualities similar to what the UNESCO biosphere reserve program seeks in terms of its goals.

These features align closely with stated principles of biosphere reserves:

- Forest Park acts as a living laboratory for scientific investigation into the protection and stewardship of land, water, and biodiversity. Its management practices for a city park are leading-edge.
- Research is currently being conducted on the park's watersheds, birds, mammals, fisheries, amphibians, reptiles, pollinators, lichens, fungi, mosses, and much more.
- Since its creation, the park has encouraged a connection between all people and nature. It fosters a special sense of place.
- In terms of ecosystem services, Forest Park offers the city of Portland its greatest hope for carbon sequestration. It is a place that can help society cope with climate change by cleaning its air and cooling the urban region.
- Forest Park's watersheds are the cleanest in the city and give health to the ailing Willamette River.

For all of these reasons, Portland's Forest Park manifests the capacity, natural assets, and public merit to become a model for a new and vital program — *Urban Biodiversity Reserves.*

As an author and wildlife biologist who has studied Forest Park for forty years, and one who continues to be filled with wonder each time I enter this forest, it is my hope that all who love this park will help realize the goal to designate it the nation's first urban biodiversity reserve and to inspire their creations around the world.

Bibliography

Adams, L.W., and L. E. Dove. 1989. *Wildlife Reserves and Corridors in the Urban Environment: A Guide to Ecological Landscape Planning and Resource Conservation.* Columbia, MD: National Institute for Urban Wildlife.

Blackburn, M., and R. G. Hatfield. 2020. *Pollinators in Forest Park: Pollinator Monitoring in the BPA and PGE Powerline Corridors.* With past contributions from Katie Hietala-Henschell. Report to Portland Parks and Recreation. Portland, OR: The Xerces Society for Invertebrate Conservation.

Bureau of Environmental Services, City of Portland (BES). 2019. *Portland Area Watershed Monitoring and Assessment Program (PAWMAP): Report on the First Four Years of Data.* (FY 2010–11 to FY 2013–14.)

Bureau of Environmental Services. City of Portland. (BES). Forthcoming. *Progress Report on the Evaluation of the Effects of Urban Land Use on Stream Health in Portland Watersheds.*

Bureau of Environmental Services. City of Portland (BES). 2005. *Framework for Integrated Management of Watershed Health: Portland Watershed Management Plan.*

Corkran, Charlotte C., and Chris Thoms. 2020. *Amphibians of Oregon, Washington and British Columbia.* Edmonton, Alberta: Lone Pine Publishing.

Deal, R. L., and C. A. Harrington, eds. 2006. *Red Alder—A State of Knowledge.* General Technical Report PNW-GTR-669. Portland, OR: US Department of Agriculture, Pacific Northwest Research Station.

Deshler, John. 2012. *Forest Park Wildlife Report.* Portland, OR: Portland Parks and Recreation.

Deshler, John. 2020. "Northern Pygmy Owl Nesting Ecology in Northwestern Oregon." *The Wilson Journal of Ornithology* 132, no. 2.

Forest Park Committee. 1976. *A Management Plan for Forest Park.* (As further revised by Council action November 10, 1976, and amended by Friends of Forest Park, December 21, 1989.) Portland, OR.

Forest Park Trails Policy. 1992. Prepared for Mike Lindberg, commissioner of Public Affairs, and Charles Jordan, director of Portland Parks and Recreation. May 12, 1992. Portland, OR.

Franklin, J. F., et al. *Ecological Characteristics of Old-growth Douglas Fir Forests.* USDA Forest Service General Technical Report. PNW-118. 1981.

Franklin, J. F., et al. *Natural Vegetation of Oregon and Washington.* USDA Forest Service General Technical Report. PNW-8. 1980.

Franklin, J. F., K. Norman Johnson, and Debora L. Johnson. 2018. *Ecological Forest Management.* Long Grove, IL: Waveland Press.

Hawksworth, David, and Martin Grube. 2020. "Lichens Redefined as Complex Ecosystems." *The New Phytologist* 227, no. 5 (September): 1281–1283.

Houle, M. C. 1990. *Wild About the City: Phase One of the West Hills Wildlife Corridor Study.* Prepared for the Multnomah County Division of Planning and Development. Portland, OR.

Jabr, Ferris. 2020. "The Social Life of Forests." *New York Times Magazine.* December 2, 2020.

Kriegh, LeeAnn. 2020. *The Nature of Portland.* Bend, OR: Tempo Press.

Maser, Chris. 1998. *Mammals of the Pacific Northwest: From the Coast to the High Cascades.* Corvallis, OR: Oregon State University Press.

McCune, Bruce, and Linda Geiser. 2009. *Macrolichens of the Pacific Northwest.* 2nd edition. Corvallis, OR: Oregon State University Press.

McCune, Bruce, and Martin Hutten. 2018. *Common Mosses of Western Oregon and Washington.* Corvallis, OR: Wild Blueberry Media.

Minnerath, A., M. Vaughan, and E. Mäder. 2014. *Maritime Northwest Citizen Science Monitoring Guide for Native Bees and Butterflies.* 2nd edition. Portland, OR: The Xerces Society.

Munger, T. T. 1960. *History of Portland's Forest Park.* The Friends of Forest Park and Portland Parks and Recreation.

Noss, R. F. 1987. "Protecting Natural Areas in Fragmented Landscapes." *Natural Areas Journal* 7:2–13.

Olmsted, J. C., and F. L. Olmsted Jr. 1903. *Report of the Park Board.* Portland, OR.

Orloff, Chet. 1980. *Willamette Heights Portland Oregon: A History.* Master's thesis, Portland State University.

Pojar, Jim, and Andy MacKinnon. 2016. *Plants of the Pacific Northwest.* Edmonton, Alberta: Lone Pine Publishing.

Portland Parks and Recreation: Bureau of Planning. 1995. *Forest Park: Natural Resources Management Plan.* Ordinance no. 168509. Adopted by City Council February 8, 1995.

Qing Li. 2018. *Forest Bathing: The Science of Shinrin-Yoku.* New York City, NY: Viking Press.

Spies, Thomas, and Sally Duncan. 2009. *Old-Growth in a New World.* Washington, D.C.: Island Press.

Spribille, Toby, et al. 2016. "Basidiomycete Yeasts in the Cortex of Ascomycete Macrolichens." *Science* 353 (6298): 488–492.

St. John, Alan D. 2002. *Reptiles of the Northwest*. Edmonton, Alberta: Lone Pine Publishing.

Trimble, D. E. 1963. *Geology of Portland, Oregon and Adjacent Areas*. Geological Survey Bulletin 1119. Portland, OR.

Trudell, Steve, and Joe Ammirati. 2009. *Mushrooms of the Pacific Northwest*. Portland, OR: Timber Press.

Turner, Mark, and Phyllis Gustafson. 2006. *Wildflowers of the Pacific Northwest*. Portland, OR: Timber Press.

Wilson, E. O. 1988. *Biodiversity*. Washington, DC: National Academy Press.

Zimmer, Carl. 2019. "Birds are Vanishing from North America." *New York Times*. September 22, 2019.

APPS AND LINKS FOR WILDLIFE AND PLANTS OF FOREST PARK

Lichens
Oregon Wildflower Search [free app]
Common Macrolichens of the Pacific Northwest [link]: lichens.twinferntech.net/pnw/

Mosses
Oregon Wildflower Search [free app]

Mushrooms
MatchMaker Mushrooms of the Pacific Northwest [free app]
svims.ca/council/matchmaker.htm [link]

Salamanders, Amphibians, Mammals, Reptiles
Oregon Department of Fish and Wildlife [link]: myodfw.com/wildlife-viewing/species/salamanders

Flowers, Shrubs, Trees, Ferns, and Grasses
Oregon Wildflower Search [free app]
Consortium of Pacific Northwest Herbaria [link]: pnwherbaria.org/index.php

Birds
Merlin Bird Id by Cornell [free app]
Audubon Bird Guide [free app]
iBird Pro Guide to Birds [paid app]
Sibley Birds 2nd edition [paid app]

Species Identification for Photographs

Unless otherwise noted, all species identification photos by John Thompson.

Index

Page numbers in **bold** type indicate photos